READING
AND
UNDERSTANDING:
Teaching from the Perspective
of Artificial Intelligence

PSYCHOLOGY OF READING

A series of volumes edited by **Rand Spiro**

SPIRO, BRUCE, and BREWER ● *Theoretical Issues in Reading Comprehension*

SCHANK ● *Reading and Understanding: Teaching from the Perspective of Artificial Intelligence*

READING
AND
UNDERSTANDING:
Teaching from the Perspective
of Artificial Intelligence

Roger C. Schank
Yale University

LEA LAWRENCE ERLBAUM ASSOCIATES, PUBLISHERS
1982   Hillsdale, New Jersey

Copyright © 1982 by Lawrence Erlbaum Associates, Inc.
All rights reserved. No part of this book may be reproduced in
any form, by photostat, microform, retrieval system or any other
means, without the prior written permission of the publisher.

Lawrence Erlbaum Associates, Inc., Publishers
365 Broadway
Hillsdale, New Jersey 07642

Library of Congress Cataloging in Publication Data

Schank, Roger C., 1946–
    Reading and understanding.

    Bibliography: p.
    Includes indexes.
    1. Reading. 2. Reading comprehension.
3. Artificial intelligence. 4. Memory. I. Title.
LB1050.S22   372.4   81-9915
ISBN 0-89859-169-4   AACR2

Printed in the United States of America

For Hana

Contents

Preface

1. **The Elements of Comprehension**   **1**
   The Perspective of Computers   1
   What to Teach   4
   Knowledge and Reading   5
   What Does One Do When One Reads?   5
   Inference-Making   9
   Memory   10
   Event-Connection   11
   What the Child Brings to Reading   12
   Early Language Learning   13
   After Age Two   14
   An Aside About Adult Knowledge   15
   A Child's Knowledge of the World   18
   Prediction Based Upon Knowledge   22

2. **First Steps in Teaching Reading**   **25**
   Predictions   25
   Teaching a Child to Predict   30
   Word Recognition   32
   Familiar Signs   33
   The Alphabet   34
   Manipulating Letters   37
   Putting it All Together   39
   Syntactic/Semantic Prediction   40
   The Rationale for the Sentence Game   42

The Stage is Set   45
Learning New Words   45
On With the Lesson   46

3. **Memory and Comprehension**   **49**
    Decoupling Reading and Language   49
    Recognition Versus Recall Memory   51
    Memory and Reading   52
    Knowing How Versus Knowing That   54
    What Can Go Wrong in Comprehension   56
    Summary   61

4. **Language and Memory**   **63**
    What's Relevant   63
    Words   64
    Representation of Meaning   67
    Conceptual Rules   68
    Conceptual Categories   68
    Actions   70
    Actions Versus States   74
    Paraphrases and Cononical Forms   77
    Similarity of Expression: The Basic Actions   80
    Other Basic Actions   85
    The Understanding of Language   89

5. **Early Reading Instruction:**
    Predictions from Language   **91**
    Predicting Objects   92
    Directions and Recipients   95
    Results and Reasons   96

6. **Background Knowledge: Scripts**   **99**
    What Materials to Select   99
    Scripts   100
    Script Interactions   106
    The Use of Scripts in Teaching Reading   107
    Material Selection and Scripts   108
    Summary   110

7. **Stories for Children: The Use of Scripts**   **111**
    Using a Script to Design a Story   111
    Stage 1: Reading Connected Text   114
    Stage 2: Enablements   115
    Stage 3: Assessing a Goal   116
    Stage 4: Beginning a Real Story: Script Failures   117
    Stage 5: Script Interferences   118
    Summary   118
    Teaching Scripts   119
    Acquiring Scripts   119

8. **More Background Knowledge: Plans and Goals**   **125**
    The Elements of Planning   128
    Planning   128
    Import of Plans   130
    Goals   131
    Goal Precedences   138
    Goals and Beliefs   140
    Summary   142

9. **Stories for Children: Using Plans and Goals**   **143**
    Stage 1: Connected Text   144
    Stage 2: Enablements   146
    Stage 3: Assessing a Goal   147
    Stage 4: Plan Failure and Goal Blockage   149
    Stage 5: Counterplanning and Goal Competition   149
    Summary   151

10. **What Not to Teach**   **153**
    Current Tools Used to Teach Reading   153
    Using What a Child Knows   157
    Decoupling   158
    Syllables   159
    Prefixes, Suffixes, and Compound Words   160
    Teaching New Vocabulary   161
    Compound Words   164
    Prefixes and Suffixes Again   166
    Summing Up   167

11. **The Context Method**   **169**
Review   169
The Teaching of Language   170
Material a Child Already Knows   171
Material a Child Will Never Need to Know   172
Material Unrelated But Useful   173
Material That is Part of the Context Reading   174
The Context Method   176
Summing Up   178

12. **Commencement: How It All Works**   **181**
Modeling a Reader   182
An Example   185

References   195

Preface

When my daughter was four years old I taught her to read. She had loved books from the time she was introduced to them at the age of two months. At first, they were objects to be mouthed. Later they were the source of pretty pictures and the warm feelings derived from sitting on a parent's lap. Still later they were the source of fun stories and the reward of her parent's appreciation when she started to recite books that she had memorized.

When she learned to read, her love of reading increased. She read a book a day at one point. At this writing, Hana is eight years old, and is in the fourth grade. She still loves to read. She reads for a half hour every night before she goes to bed, and often reads at other times during the day. She almost never watches television. Outside of sports, reading is her favorite activity. Why do I bother to mention all this here? Because, if you ask Hana what she likes least about school, she will tell you "Language." In fact, she detests "Language." She finds it boring and she feels she learns nothing from it.

When she first told me about this, I asked to see her reading workbooks. I was astounded at what I found there. There was good reason for her to hate "Language."

Throughout most of my life, I have been involved in teaching computers to read. I have worked extensively on determining the nature of the human reading process, so that we could get computers to simulate it. I never thought a great deal about how children were taught to read. I assumed that it was being done in a reasonable fashion. And perhaps it was, given what has been understood about the process of reading.

But, we now know a great deal about reading that has not in any way influenced how reading is taught. It is not surprising that our research has had no effect, since people who work in Artificial Intelligence are in the field of Computer Science, and usually have little contact with educators or people whose research is on how to teach reading to children.

Fortuitously, Rand Spiro, a psychologist whose specialty is reading, spent the 1979–1980 academic year with us at Yale. He suggested that I write this book.

Various people have been helpful in early drafts of this book. In particular, I wish to thank Rand Spiro, Ann Drinan, Diane Schank, and Mark Burstein for their help. Rand Spiro was especially helpful in attempting to get me to see the world from a teacher's perspective, although I confess to have probably not achieved full understanding. Ann Drinan has been a right (write?) arm to me in much of what I have written in the last two years. She worked a great deal on this book in an attempt to change my academic style into one that is more comprehensible.

I also wish to acknowledge the support of the Advanced Research Projects Agency of the Department of Defense, the Office of Naval Research, and the National Science Foundation, all of whom have helped fund the Artificial Intelligence Project at Yale.

Lastly, the theory and programs used as background in this book were collaborative efforts. Many of the ideas presented here on scripts, plans, and goals, were originally worked out in a book entitled *Scripts Plans Goals and Understanding* that I wrote with Bob Abelson. Various students contributed to those ideas and subsequent ideas, many of which have been realized here. In particular, Bob Wilensky, Jaime Carbonell, Richard Cullingford, Wendy Lehnert, Larry Birnbaum, and Mike Lebowitz worked on computer programs that helped to realize and expand the ideas presented here. I thank them and many other members of the Yale Artificial Intelligence Project for the stimulation they have provided me throughout the years.

This book was written partially in Barbados but mostly in Jamaica while I was on leave from Yale. It was completed in New Haven, Connecticut.

Roger C. Schank

1 The Elements of Comprehension

THE PERSPECTIVE OF COMPUTERS

What specific rules do we try to impart when we teach someone to read? What does it mean for someone to understand? Where are the trouble spots in understanding? These and similar questions are crucial issues in planning an effective strategy for the teaching of reading.

In the past few years we have learned a great deal about reading processes from what may seem a rather unlikely source—computers. This derives from a decade of research in programming computers to read English. One might ask, "What could such an effort have to do with teaching children to read?" This is indeed a reasonable question. It was by no means obvious, at the outset of research on making machines intelligent (a field of research called Artificial Intelligence, henceforth AI), that we would learn about people from those efforts.

But gradually, researchers in AI learned that the intelligent tasks that they wished computers to emulate were much more complex than they had originally imagined. What a person does when reading is far more complex, according to a great many measures, than what one does when playing chess. It began to be clear to AI researchers that if they were to enable computers to read, they would have to design computer programs that were simulations of how people read. There was little reason to believe that there were many other or more preferable ways to read apart from the human method, so AI researchers concentrated their efforts on determining what processes people use when they read.

The AI methods used were by no means the conventional experimental methods of that time. Rather, AI researchers design a detailed step-by-step procedure (this is called an algorithm in computer parlance) that pinpoints every single thing that must be done by a reader. The researcher designs these algorithms to coincide at every possible point with what is known to be true of people in a given situation.

To illustrate a small part of how one can determine what a person must be doing when reading, consider the following example. Suppose a person was asked to read the sentence

Shakespeare wrote Hamlet

and was then given a reading comprehension test. If one of the questions on the test were "Who was the author of Hamlet?" we would expect our reader to answer correctly if he had understood what he had read. But how would he be able to do this? That is, what is the exact procedure that would enable him to answer this question?

The obvious procedures do not necessarily work. For example, it is possible to design an algorithm that matches the phrase "was the author of" with "wrote." Early computer programs actually did attempt to answer questions in this way. However, such procedures proved inadequate when "wrote" was used in sentences such as "John wrote Mary" or when "was the author of" was used in sentences such as "Babe Ruth was the author of the book on how to hit home runs."

It seems clear that people do not understand or answer questions by such simple matching procedures. Then what do they do? They encode what they read (or hear) into a *representation* of the meaning of what they have read (or heard). Humans who can understand a langauge have learned certain rules by which they can extract meanings from sentences. These meanings are then stored in their memories in a form that is different from the original form of the sentence that they heard.

No matter how events described by sentences are stored in memory, they cannot be stored in terms of whatever words may have been used in those sentences. There are a great many ways to describe an event, but the event remains the same regardless of the description. Similarly, memory's encoding of that event is the same regardless of the description. Thus, any meaning representation used by the mind must be non-lingual, involving pure meaning elements only. No matter what lexical form is chosen to express a particular thought, there will be only one conceptual meaning representation stored in memory. This explains why people who speak two or more languages fluently sometimes forget which language they are using; the concepts they wish to express are stored in neither language in their memories.

If this non-linguistic meaning representation did not exist, we would be unable to solve the "Shakespeare" question posed above. Clearly, both the question and the original statement of the Shakespeare sentence must be decoded into a form that represents the meaning of each in virtually identical formats. To put this another way, the meaning element "to author by writing" must be used in a representation of both the sentence and the question.

To a large extent, the task of programming computers to read has involved finding the set of meaning elements to which language refers, finding the rule for decoding sentences into those elements, and finally, encoding those elements into sentences. For our purposes, an important part of reading is the decoding of sentences into a representation of their meaning.

But, as AI researchers found out, reading is much more than that. Programming computers to decode sentences into representations of their meaning did not lead to understanding in any deep sense. Real understanding requires a complex knowledge of the world and a range of experiences. Current research in AI involves enabling computers to have and use such complex world knowledge. How they have accomplished this is also extremely relevant to teaching children to read.

However, it is not my intention here to discuss computers. The theories of reading described here have already been explored in great detail by AI researchers, whose interests diverge from those tho whom this book is addressed. Nevertheless, what we have learned about language and reading from AI has many applications, one of the most significant being what it tells us about how we can most effectively teach reading.

WHAT TO TEACH

We can specify two distinct aspects of the reading process that have consequences for the teaching of reading. The first is the association of a sound with a given set of letters. Is "sight" or "phonics" is the best method for associating symbol and sound? I do not believe that this is an either-or situation, and will discuss this further in Chapter 2.

The teaching of word recognition takes place in the early grades. By the second grade, most children can read simple words in isolation. From that point on, many school systems invest most of their effort in the second aspect of the reading process. It is hard to put a name to this second part; many schools call it "Language" or "Language Arts." Lumped together under this rubric are such diverse items as spelling, syllabification, alphabetization, and many others. I hope to persuade the reader that many of the items usually included in this second phase of reading instruction ought to be separated from what I believe actually needs to be taught about reading after the initial skills have been learned. For now, the issue is to determine what needs to be taught in this second phase. What is it that a child, who has learned how to associate sound and symbol, must learn in order to be a capable reader? The answer to that question takes up most of this book. An effective reader is one who has a strong desire to read. Comprehension is what drives reading, and in the end, what makes word recognition possible. It is comprehension that must be fostered but, ironically, comprehension is the least understood of the phenomena that comprise reading. In the major part of this book, I will concentrate on comprehension and suggest how it might be better taught.

KNOWLEDGE AND READING

One reason it is difficult to teach reading in the first grade is that a child of six or seven has considerable knowledge about the world and about language. The crucial determinant in what can be read by anyone, child or adult, is the amount of background knowledge they possess to help them determine the meaning of what they are reading. A child of six or seven is relatively sophisticated in his knowledge of the world. He may understand some of the intricacies of professional football, how a movie is made, the dynamics of social relationships, divorce, how a car works, how to build a table, even some rudiments of politics. Yet the child who knows all these things is usually asked to read sentences far below his intellectual level. He will probably be bored to death with it.

This may be remedied to some extent by offering the child more interesting or relevant texts. But, in the beginning, these texts will still be considerably beneath him with respect to knowledge, because learning to read must begin at the beginning. It is preferable, I believe, to teach reading at an age when the child is not bored by the simple things of the world. Progress in teaching the child reading must keep pace with the absorption of world knowledge. If one progresses significantly faster than the other, a child may encounter great difficulties in learning to read.

WHAT DOES ONE DO WHEN ONE READS

What does one do during the reading process? Since reading is, after all, primarily comprehension, the key question to ask is what is a person doing when he is attempting to "understand"?

A large part of the understanding process is the attempt to make explicit what is implicit in a sentence, or a situation in general. Language is a means of conveying information. But frequently what is expressed in an actual sentence is only a small part of what the speaker wishes to convey. Often, much of the intended information is left implicit. It is thus the job of our memories to fill in what has been left out.

Thus when we hear someone say that they like a book, it is our memory processes that are responsible for determining that this probably means that they liked reading the book, as opposed to holding it, for example. When we hear that John likes Mary, in certain contexts we will understand that he might want to be with Mary, or might ask Mary for a date. Such additional information comes from our memories and is incorporated into our understanding of what we hear. We learn to make guesses or predictions about what we hear, in order to help us fill in the details of what we have been told. In reading, these same "guesses" apply. That is why teaching a child to be literal-minded when he reads is often a great mistake.

This predicted information also tells us what *not* to think, in regard to what we have been told. Notice that the expectation that John will want to read Mary does not come to mind. But what is the actual surface difference between "John likes books" and "John likes Mary"? The difference between them is found at the meaning level, but it is not explained solely by saying that there are two different senses of "like" here. To clarify this problem, consider the following simple, everyday exchange:

John: I need some aspirin for my cold.

Mary: Why don't you try Vitamin C instead?

Since Mary has given the response here, we can begin to think about the process of language by examining the processing Mary would need to have done in order to say what she did.

The first process in understanding is called *analysis*. Mary's first task is to analyze what John has said. The result of her analysis will be her perceptions of the meaning of John's sentence. What subprocesses make up analysis?

The first subprocess is *lexical look-up*. To assign a meaning to the words John has spoken, Mary must determine the meanings of them individually. To do this people employ a kind of mental dictionary. This dictionary has several properties that make it quite different from an ordinary dictionary found on a bookshelf. The dictionary available to the mind clearly cannot contain English defintions of words. For one thing, the definitions of words given in ordinary dictionaries are circular. Words are defined in terms of other words, which are themselves defined in terms of the original words. This method may work well for lexicographers, but for use by the mind, it would work very poorly. Our mental dictionaries contain what we shall call *concepts*. One such concept is an abstract idea of a thing. For example, the word "chair," when looked up in our mental dictionaries, will call up the concept of a chair. Everyone's concept of a chair will not be the same, of course. Some people see a chair in their mind's eye; others do not visualize at all. But whatever this concept looks like internally, it uniquely specifies what a chair's description and function.

Another significant difference between conventional dictionaries and mental ones is that the latter must do more than simply define the word. Mental dictionaries must also give information to help the analysis process on its way. Thus the purpose of mental dictionaries is different than the purpose of ordinary ones. A printed dictionary tells its user the meaning of a word he does not know in terms of ones he does know. A mental dictionary tells its user what he knows about a word. Part of what a person knows about a word is what it means—the concept or group of concepts to which the word refers. Another equally important part of what a person knows about a word is how that word is used—what other words are likely to be found in sentences containing the word that has been looked up, how those other words related to that word, and so on.

After lexical look-up is completed for the first word in a sentence, a new subprocess is begun. Before we explain this subprocess, it is important to emphasize the significance of the last statement. It would be nice if every mental process succeeded every other mental process neatly in turn. But the fact is that human language processes do not, and in fact could not, work in this way. We cannot look up the meaning of each word in a sentence one at a time and, when we have finished looking them all up, proceed to examine the sentence as a whole. Each word's meaning affects the meaning of the words surrounding it. Thus, to decide on the correct choice of a meaning for a word, it is necessary to understand it in terms of the partially composed meaning of the entire sentence. For example, the meaning of "straw" is different in each of the next two sentences, as is the meaning of "plane" in the following two:

Sip your soda with a straw.

Lie down on that straw

I took the plane to New York.

I used the plane in the garage.

Words have multiple possible meanings. Because of this we can never simply say: "The meaning of this word is such and such." The context that surrounds a word determines its meaning. This is true to such an extent that even in the examples given above, we can reverse the meanings of the word "plane" simply by supplying a new sentence that provides a different context.

John needs to do some woodworking.

I took the plane to New York.

How did you get to New York?

I used the plane in the garage.

Every language process, therefore, is working simultaneously. No one process can work in isolation from the others. However, since we cannot write about every process at the same time, we shall have to be more sequential in our presentation than is actually true of people's thinking processes.

Let's return to our earlier example:

John: I need some aspirin for my cold.

Mary: Why don't you try Vitamin C instead?

The next subprocess of analysis, after lexical look-up, is *event identification*. Any declarative statement expresses either a description of the state of the world, or an event that has taken or will take place. The process of event identification is the process of fitting the concepts that have been obtained through lexical look-up into an event or state description. Thus the word "I" in the example above is first identified by lexical look-up as the concept of the speaker, "John." The subprocess of event identification hypothesizes at this point that "John" is a likely candidate to be the actor in an event, among other things.

Analysis can only rarely be completed entirely by itself. Usually, while the event identification part of the analysis process is being attempted, a second process of *inference-making* must begin.

INFERENCE-MAKING

After running through the analysis process, the event and states that Mary can identify from John's statement about his cold are:

state of the world: John has a cold.

intended event: actor: John

object: aspirin

Clearly, much more is being expressed in the sentence "I need some aspirin   for my cold." What other processes are necessary to explicate what is implicit?

First of all, our attempt at event identification has not been completely successful. In fact, we have found no action for our event! The only verb we have is "need." But "need" does not tell us what John intends to *do* with the aspirin. This is the province of the process of *inference-making*.

Inference-making is the process of making best guesses about what a speaker must have meant, apart from what he said explicitly. So, although the sentence does not say that John intends to put the aspirin in his mouth and swallow it, that is a very good guess (though it may turn out to be wrong). One of the subprocesses that make up inference-making is the process of *filling in the blanks*. What we have done in the above inference is to fill in the probable unstated event that John intends.

Another subprocess of inference-making is the process of *goal identi-*

fication. When we are told that someone wants to do something, we usually ask why. To convince yourself of this, consider a story like: "John loved Mary. Somebody mugged Mary in the park. When John heard about this he was satisfied." It is difficult here to explain John's reaction. The only way we can do so is by imagining some of John's and Mary's goals and seeking some explanation of how mugging may have been in concert with some goal of John's. The story is peculiar because the proposition that the mugging could have a good effect is peculiar. Of course, there would have been no problem had "was satisfied" been replaced by "cried." But in the latter case we would have no conscious remembrance of searching our memories for the connectedness of the goals and actions of the characters in the story, because crying is not an unusual response to the situation. But, conscious or not, an important part of the understanding process is the identification of goals, and the recognition that goals are connected to the actions intended to achieve them.

So, if we can figure out *why* someone wants to do something, we can begin to understand his actions. If we cannot find the why, we are often baffled by what he does. The answer to why John wants the aspirin is obvious. He clearly believes that taking aspirin will either cure his cold or at least assuage its symptoms. The fact that all this is obvious leaves us with a very important question. How do we know it? What processes does the mind go through in its attempt to discover all these obvious (but unstated) facts? To find these answers, the mind consults its *Memory*.

MEMORY

Memory is not a separate enclave, divorced from the processes of inference-making or analysis. In fact, each of those processes needs to consult memory as a repository of information. Memory provides the answer to: "What does 'I' or 'aspirin' mean for the lexical look-up process?", as well as the answer to: "What do you do with aspirin?" for the inference-making process. Memory is thus a giver of information to process rather than a process itself.

One of the kinds of information present in memory is called a *belief.* A belief is an attitude or a feeling a person has towards an event or state of the world. People have beliefs about many kinds of things. As under-standers, we use or consult these beliefs when we decide what is proper to do, as well as when we attempt to decide why someone is doing something.

Other kinds of information available in memory include: facts, knowledge about episodes in one's own life, knowledge about history and current events, etc. In other words, we understand everything we hear in terms of what we already know and have stored in our memories.

EVENT-CONNECTION

The next component process in understanding is called *event-connection.* In event-connection, we attempt to find out if the new input we have received fits in with any beliefs, contradictory facts, or other information that will help to explain, or connect together, the new event or states of the world of which we have just been informed.

In order for Mary to understand John's statement about needing an aspirin, it is necessary for her to attempt to establish a connection between John's cold and his taking aspirin. One method of doing this is to consult memory for a belief that connects the two. A relevant belief here might be:

Taking aspirin relieves cold symptoms.

Finding this belief, Mary will then have understood this sentence to mean:

John has a cold.

He intends to put aspirin in his mouth and swallow it.

He believes this will relieve his cold symptoms.

He does not now have the aspirin.

All of these components, and more that are beyond the scope of this book, contribute to the process of comprehension. Every one of them is a crucial part of what we do when we read. With this as background, we are now ready to consider how we might best teach a child to comprehend new information which happens to be in written form.

WHAT THE CHILD BRINGS TO READING

Children do not enter the first grade as empty-headed beings. By the age of six, children speak their language very well. And, although they may be illiterate, they are not ignorant. They possess large vocabularies, know a great deal about the syntactic structures of their language, and have a tremendous amount of information about the world.

One of the very important tasks of the reading instructor is to assess what a child currently knows so that he can build upon it. Note that here I am referring to a child's knowledge of the outside world rather than his knowledge of either reading or language. Actually the problem I am referring to can be understood by considering many other tasks that require understanding but have nothing to do with reading. For example, a six year old will only understand the barest parts of a movie that is not intended specifically for him because he does not have the requisite knowledge of the world.

Confounding this problem of knowledge assessment for the teacher of reading is the problem of assessing what a child knows of his language. A child who speaks well, for example, will have implicitly learned a great deal about the rules of his language. For example, it may seem quite reasonable to teachers of reading to teach children about words ending in "-ly" or "-er," but most children in the early grades already use such endings in their speech. Furthermore, they understand words that have such endings. They do not have *explicit* knowledge of the meanings of those endings, but that does not mean they lack that knowledge *implicitly*. That is, the kind of knowledge the child needs to help him read words with those endings is already present. There is no reason to teach a child to have explicit knowledge of what he knows implicitly.

The problem then is to assess what children need to be taught with respect to their language. In doing so we must determine what they bring to the reading situation. What do they know and what do they need to be taught?

EARLY LANGUAGE LEARNING

Children begin to learn their language at birth. They begin to differentiate sounds in their language and commence to babble in those sounds. For the purposes of reading, we will concentrate not on sounds but on words. The first words tend to appear in children between nine and thirteen months of age (Benedict 1967). But this is not the beginning of the language process. Until the age of nine months the child is not sitting dormant waiting for language to begin.

We referred earlier to the meaning elements that are used to decode and encode language. During the first nine months of life, a child is learning these meaning elements. He is learning to "grasp," to "give," to "move his body in a desired direction"; to "apply a force to something," to "attempt to communicate," and so on. As we shall see in Chapter 3, these are some of the basic meaning elements that he will use of the rest of his life. When he learns words they will be learned in terms of these elements. That is, he will learn the meaning of words because he already knows the meaning part, which allows him to attend to the word itself.

A simple example of this is seen in the "giving game" that all children play around the age of nine months. They happily trade possession of a toy with a parent. From this game they first learn the concepts of possession and the transfer of possession. Later, because they have learned this meaning element, together with its associated parts (i.e., a possession, an object, and an action—a transfer of possession—performed upon that object), they are ready to attend to the word that describes the composite whole. After a while when the parent says "give" they know to begin the game. But, prior to the word-based imitation is gestural-based imitation. That is, the meaning element is learned first, the word second.

Words are learned in general in this manner. First, a situation is set up, such as throwing a ball or putting blocks in a stack, and then, from this well defined situtation, the child learns the relationship of the objects and actions involved. He learns to predict how things will turn out. He becomes upset when the normal routine is altered. In other words, his conceptual apparatus is extremely complex and sophisticated before he learns the actual words that describe aspects of the situation with which he is already familiar.

Since the meanings of words are very complex, and usually situationally-based, there really cannot be any other way for a child to learn new vocabulary. He does not learn one word in terms of another. He learns words in terms of a situation and in terms of predictions and expectations that he has already made about that situation. Such situations form the basis of his internal mental definitions for the word he has learned.

The key point then is this. A child learns words in terms of situations that he already understands, and in terms of knowledge that he has already acquired. At any point, a child has more knowledge than he has vocabulary available to express that knowledge. Give him vocabulary at the right level and he will learn very quickly. *The key to teaching vocabulary is the assessment of the child's knowledge.*

AFTER AGE TWO

By age two, the average child has acquired a vocabulary that is useful for understanding and describing the world around him (Wetstone and Friedlander, 1973; Selfridge, 1980). He may not utter all the words he knows, however. Comprehension precedes speech production. This is an important point to keep in mind when we discuss reading in more detail. Children have a much more sophisticated understanding of the world around them than they are capable of expressing verbally at any given time.

Between the ages of two and three, a child begins to combine the words he knows into sentences. Remember that he has been understanding simple sentences, usually in the form of commands or questions, for some time. His early sentences describe the world around him or are used by him to get what he needs. Sentences such as "big dog," "want milk," and "see nice man" are common. By age three, the child's vocabulary has expanded to the point where he has words to describe all the objects in his environment that are relevant to him, all of his own actions and those actions of others around him that he can understand, and various states of the world that are of import to him.

By the time a child enters school, he speaks a simplified form of adult English. His vocabulary is large, but it is constrained by lack of experience with the world. A child cannot have words for situations, events, or objects, that he has not experienced.

AN ASIDE ABOUT ADULT KNOWLEDGE

What does an adult know that a child of six does not? On the face of it, this seems like a silly question. An adult has a sophisticated knowledge of the whole world; a child understands only a small part of what is present in his immediate environment. To rephrase the question then, what does an adult know that enables him to read that a six year old does not know? One obvious answer is the orthography. That is, a child of six doesn't know that a group of letters can indicate a word, or what word any group does indicate. But what else?

The answer can be found in some of the previously referred to research in Artificial Intelligence, particularly with respect to the kinds of knowledge that computers need in order to understand stories. The summary of these results are that computers had to know how to:

1. Make Simple Inferences
2. Establish Causal Connections
3. Recognize Stereotyped Situations (scripts)
4. Predict and Generate Plans
5. Track People's Goals
6. Recognize Thematic Relationships between Individuals and Society
7. Employ Beliefs about the World in Understanding
8. Access and Utilize Raw Facts

These eight kinds of knowledge roughly categorize what an adult knows about the world. A child in the first grade has all this kind of knowledge too, but in a simplified form. Since reading depends upon this knowledge, effective reading instruction demands that we pay attention to this dependency.

The eight types of knowledge referred to above help a reader to interpret what he hears, sees, and reads, which in turn help him determine the import of what he has read. To see how this works, let's consider the knowledge involved, according to these eight categories, in reading a simple story:

> John hated his boss. He went to the bank and got twenty dollars. He bought a gun. The next day at work he decided to ask his boss for a raise. But John was so upset by his own plan that he told his boss he was sick and went home and cried.

This is a simple story, on the surface. The words are easy and most third graders would have very little difficulty reading the story out loud. Yet very few of them would feel they had understood it. Beneath the surface of some simple words are some complicated ideas that require an adult's understanding of the world to interpret. To analyze this story completely in terms of the eight categories of knowledge presented above would take too much time and would be far from the point of this book. Let me illustrate just some of the ways in which each of these eight categories comes into play.

1. Inferences. In order to understand a sentence fully, it is necessary to draw conclusions from that sentence about the things that were not explicitly stated but which nevertheless are true. People are rarely aware that they are making an inference at any given time. They are much more aware that they have made one when that inference is violated or in error for some reason.

Some inferences necessary for understanding the above story are:

a. After buying the gun, John has the gun,
   i.e., buying implies having.
b. The gun cost twenty dollars,
   i.e., buying requires money.
c. John intends to use the gun,
   i.e., you buy something for its eventual use.
d. John will threaten or possibly shoot someone,
   i.e., functional objects (e.g., guns) are used for their function.

2. Causal Connections. Adults have an understanding of how one event relates to another. There are many different kinds of causal relations (see Schank, 1975). Adults attempt to determine the causal relationships inherent in what they are trying to understand. (This category and the others described below can all be seen as different varieties of inference.) One causal relationship in the above story is:

Going to the bank enabled John to get money,
   i.e., "going" can enable actions that ordinarily take place at the location arrived at.

3. Stereotyped Situation (Scripts). People have a great deal of information about stereotyped situations. In this story those that are referred to are banks, stores (implicitly—the place where John bought the gun) and offices. Understanding this story requires a working knowledge of how such scripts function. (Scripts will be discussed in detail in Chapter 5.)

4. Plan Prediction and Generation. To understand this story fully, it is necessary to postulate a set of possible plans under which John is likely to be operating. In order to postulate such plans, however, one has to be able to generate them oneself. The more that John's actions seem to the reader to fit into a coherent plan of action, the more "understandable" the story seems. This plan-creation and understanding ability is at the heart of following a story of this kind. This is precisely where a third grader will find himself severely handicapped when trying to understand the story. Even the simplest of plans is hard to follow if you have not learned *how* to follow another person's plan.

5. *Goal Tracking.* What is John going to do and why is he doing it? These are the questions that occur as we read this story. However, answering such questions requires knowing about goals such as being well treated, respected, well paid or whatever complex set of goals are reasonable to postulate in understanding this story.

6. *Thematic Relationships.* Understanding this story requires a good assessment of how an employee might feel towards a boss, and an interpretation of hatred in this context. A third grader may know what "hate" means to him, but his definition is likely to be only partially relevant here, and much of his understanding of that word may be irrelevant., Another important thematic relationship is the fear of being an outcast, immoral person, or a criminal, all of which one can imagine to be something going through John's mind.

7. *Beliefs.* We, as readers, believe certain things about what is right and wrong. If John is going to threaten his boss for a raise, or possible kill him, we view it at least as misguided, and probably terribly wrong. These beliefs about what is a correct course of action in the world are very much a part of how we understand and thus of how we read.

8. *Raw Facts.* Banks have money. Bosses give raises. Crying releases tension. Stores sell guns. All these are simple facts about the world, without which it would be hard to understand this story.

A CHILD'S KNOWLEDGE OF THE WORLD

We are now ready to return to our three year old. What does he know of the world? What, within the range of these eight kinds of knowledge, is available to him to help him understand?

1. Inferences. By age three a child can make some very simple inferences. He knows that if you put something someplace, it will be there; that if you eat, you won't be hungry anymore, and so on. Recall that the ability to make inferences is dependent upon world knowledge in the first place. So, while the basic apparatus is there by age three, the only things that a child of this age can infer are those things about which he already has a good understanding, i.e., things within his small world.

2. Causal Connections. A three year old child has a very confused view of what causes what (Piaget, 1954). At age three a child is willing to believe just about anything with respect to causality. Because of this, he often cannot make the correct causal connections in what he reads.

3. Stereotyped Situations (Scripts). Children do, on the other hand, have very sophisticated scripts. In fact, there is evidence to suggest that children are forming scripts almost from birth (Nelson, 1975, Schank and Abelson, 1977, Nelson and Gruendel, 1978). The scripts that they form are discarded or improved as the case warrants, a process that serves as one basis for learning. Thus, by age 4, a child has very good and detailed knowledge, albeit from his own point of view and experiences, of such stereotyped situations as banks, grocery stores, meal times, and restaurants.

As an example of this, consider a conversation between a Parent (P) and a four year old (C):

P: Now, I want you to tell me what happens when you go to a restaurant.
C: OK.
P: What happens in a restaurant? Start at the beginning.
C: You come in and you sit down at the table. And then the waitress comes. And she gives you a menu. And, then she takes it back and writes down your order. And then, you eat what she gave you. And then you get up from the table. And you pay the money and then you walk out of the store.

It is clear from the above (taken from Schank and Abelson, 1977) that the four year old has a very good notion of what goes on in a restaurant. Another example of this (taken from Nelson and Gruendel, 1979) is a conversation between two children about what happens in nursery school. This conversation took place while they were playing with a model of the school and some props.

> C1: School is ready.
> C2: School is ready! Uh-oh, ba-sketti-oh!
> C1: The door's closed, because it's not locked up. But you can walk in this door. (Walks person in.) And, but no one there has a (?). Not snack time, yet. First, you take your coat off.
> C2: Here I come to school, walk. The TEACHER! (Walks teacher into school.)
> C1: THEN, then you play, then you play.
> C2: This is the teacher. This is the teacher. She's looking out the window.
> C1: These guys are playing outside now. Now people are playing outside.
> C2: No, they're taking a nap now. Put'em in! They're going to take a nap now. Teacher, the teacher's rubbing her back. The Teacher's . . . rubbing . . .
> C1: She . . . this is the teacher, and she's walking outside to get something from her car. Ba-doop (walks teacher to pretend car). Get something out from her car. (Laughs.) Walk back inside. OK.
> C2: Her mother's car is broken, so let's ride in the teacher's car.
> C1: Yeah, rubbing your back, rubbing your back. (Makes teacher rub children's backs.) Ooops, school's closed!
> C2: School's closed! Wake up everybody. Time to go outside, time to go outside. WHEEE!!! (Everyone is moved outside the school.)

4. Plans. A child of three does very little planning that is not extremely simple. Consequently he cannot track someone else's plans very well. By the age of six, a child's ability to plan for himself is greatly improved, but understanding someone else's plan can still be quite difficult. Consider the following story that was read to the child who talked about restaurants, on that same day. She was then asked questions about the story. Notice that her answers indicate a strong reliance on script-based knowledge and a failure to comprehend fully the plans of the characters in the story:

> John loved Mary but she didn't want to marry him. One day, a dragon stole Mary from the castle. John got on top of his horse and killed the dragon. Mary agreed to marry him. They lived happily every after.
>
> P: Why did John kill the dragon?
> C: Cause it was mean.
> P: What was mean about it?
> C: It was hurting him.
> P: How did it hurt him?
> C: It was probably throwing fire at him.
> P: Why did Mary agree to marry John?
> C: Cause she loved him very much and he wanted very much to marry her.
> P: What was going to happen to Mary?
> C: If what?
> P: When the dragon got her?
> C: She would get dead.
> P: Why would the dragon do that?
> C: Because it wanted to eat her.
> P: How come Mary decided to marry John when she wouldn't in the beginning?
> C: That's a hard question.
> P: Well, what do you think the answer is?
> C: Because then she just didn't want him and then he argued very much and talked to her a lot about marrying her and then she got interested in marrying her, I mean him.

5. *Goals.* As with plans, a child's goals are so simple that he has almost no ability to understand that someone else might have more complex goals, much less be able to track someone else's goals. This is a very important point in considering what stories are appropriate for

children at any given age. If a child cannot understand the goals of the characters, in the deepest sense of understanding, he will not be able to follow the story he is reading, no matter how simple the vocabulary and syntax of that story.

6. Thematic Relationships. A child understands certain thematic relationships that he himself is involved in. Thus, he knows about what mothers and fathers do, for example. But, his knowledge of the role of the grocer or the bus driver is much more limited. He has only the vaguest notions about the aspects of their roles that do not relate directly to him. He may not realize that a doctor gets money for what he does, for example. Other thematic relationships such as dishonesty or malevolence, will be totally unclear to a three year old. Stories that use such relationships will be difficult for a young child to fully comprehend.

7. Beliefs. A child's beliefs are constantly changing. Here again, story understanding must relate to beliefs the child actually holds, if he is to understand a story.

8. Raw Facts. The child has quite a few of these. Here again, the same caveats apply.

PREDICTION BASED UPON KNOWLEDGE

In preparing to teach children to read, we must concentrate on their learning to comprehend the world around them. Of course, in learning to read, the child must first learn to recognize words on the printed page. After that, the fundamentals of comprehending what people are doing and why they are doing it are of more use in learning to read than any of the more traditional things taught in reading instruction. It turns out, quite happily, that the child who comprehends the world around him can use that knowledge to help in reading. This knowledge is useful in two ways. First, to understand what is new, one must understand what has come before. It is very difficult to make sense of input without a context.

Secondly, a child must learn to anticipate in order to read. He must predict words so that he can recognize them, and he must predict actions so that he can make sense of them. The reading instructor can help the child learn to make such predictions, to feel confident about his predictions, and to rely upon them.

In their desire to understand, children bring to the reading process an ability to make a wide range of predictions. A reading instructor can capitalize on this ability by helping the child make use of his predictive knowledge.

2 First Steps in Teaching Reading

PREDICTIONS

What does it mean when we say that we rely upon our ability to predict during the process of understanding? By that, I do not mean that we "know" with great certainty what will come next. Nevertheless, we do have an "idea" about it, and this idea is used by our comprehension processes in selecting alternatives. Thus our predictive abilities make our processing easier by narrowing the number of possible false paths we might choose in ambiguous circumstances. This predictive ability is useful in every single part of the comprehension process.

1. We Predict Sounds

Because we know what words are in our language, we tend to finish them in our minds before the speaker we are listening to finishes them himself. When we cannot do this, we frequently can't detect where one word ends and another begins. In understanding English, it is prediction that prevents us from confusing "I scream" with "ice cream," which are phonologically identical. It is the lack of such phonological predictions that causes children to say, "I led the pigeons to the flag" as the first line of the American pledge of allegiance. It is this inability to predict phonologically that causes us, when we are hearing a language that we do not know, to be unable to tell where one word starts and another ends. In continuous speech, spaces between words rarely exist. It is our phonological predictive abilities that help us to determine where these spaces ought to go.

2. We Predict Syntactic Units

When a sentence is being heard or read, we know the kind of word that will come next (to the extend that such syntactic determinations need to be made at all). Thus, "the big blue . . . " demands that a noun comes next. "John likes to . . . " demands a verb. These predictions can be wrong to some extent. Often what we predict does not come or comes a bit later, but even then these predictions are still very useful.

3. We Predict Semantic Classes or Words

When we hear "John took a trip to . . . " we are expecting a location. For "John hates . . . " we expect a human or an activity. The violation of these kinds of predictions are the source of a great many jokes:

Q: Do you serve crabs here?
A: We serve anybody.

On a hunting expedition we shot two bucks.
That was all the money we had.

The fact that we predict semantic classes of words, usually by context, is extremely important in understanding. The violation of such contextual predictions can make us laugh, but the lack of violation, i.e., getting what we expected, can greatly lessen our work in processing what we hear or read.

4. We Predict Word Sense from Context

When a context is set up, the problem of finding the proper sense for a word with multiple senses disappears. This point cannot be made too strongly. Word sense detection, or the disambiguation of the multiple possible meanings of a word, is one of the most fearsome problems in understanding. Words like "serve," "order," "have," "hold," "take," and so on, each have a number of different, often unrelated meanings. For example, a few of the meanings of "hit" are:

John hit the man with his fist.	"punched"
John hit the jackpot.	"did well" or "won money"
The play was a hit.	"success"
John hit the number.	"correctly selected"
John hit upon the idea.	"came up with"
The batter hit the ball.	"swung a bat at and made contact"

As understanders, we cannot possibly be working from a list of a hundred possible choices for the meaning of "hit," attempting to find the correct one. Rather we must be able to detect the correct meaning from what else has gone on before, or from what follows (i.e., from the context). This we do with ease.

John and Mary were racing.
John beat Mary.

John and Mary were angry.
John beat Mary.

The waitress went over to the table.
John paid the check.

(this one needs to be read aloud)

A Czech, a Pole and a Russian all demanded the money.
John paid the Czech.

The waitress asked which wine John would like.
John ordered the red to be brought to him.

A Russian soldier was captured by the Americans.
John ordered the Red to be brought to him.

Each of these highly ambiguous second sentences has a completely different meaning, depending on what precedes it. The fact that we never notice the second interpretation in natural situations attests to the role of prediction.

In order for computer programs to model human processes for understanding sentences such as those above, predictive procedures must be built. That is, we do not want our programs to be entertaining multiple hypotheses at once, since there is no evidence that that is what people do. Thus, we allow our programs to make only one hypothesis or prediction about what will happen next. These predictions rerank the word sense preferences according to the context that has been established. Thus when a word sense is chosen for an input, it is the one most closely identified with the prior context. The other alternatives, since they are second choices are never even noticed.

5. We Predict What Will Happen Next in a Story

It is our ability to predict what is likely to happen at any given point that allows us to understand what is happening. Prediction occurs at all levels of knowledge. The following examples illustrate the role of prediction in disambiguating intentions rather than just meanings:

John and Mary were having steak.
Mary asked John for the knife.

John was screaming at Mary and threatening to stab her.
Mary asked John for the knife.

John told Mary he loved her.
Mary gave him a kiss.

The hero brought back little Sara alive.
Mary gave him a kiss.

The man pointed a gun at Mary in a dark alley.
Mary gave him a kiss.

Here the action itself is not ambiguous. What happened in each set of sentences was identical from the point of view of what Mary did. But her feelings, the likelihood of what would happen next, and our beliefs about the situation are radically different in each case.

Thus we are predicting outcomes of events. We expect events to occur in a certain order. We predict feelings, attitudes, likely responses, and so on. When these predictions are violated we are surprised. Often such violations form the basis of a good story. (Imagine if Mary had spit at the hero above. We would then want to know more.) Writers exploit our predictive abilities when they provide a story with an unusual twist or a surprise. A great deal of humor also makes use of our penchant for making predictions.

Our ability to predict is of paramount importance in understanding. We predict nearly everything that is a part of the comprehension process. To a large extent then, prediction forms the basis of our ability to read.

Goodman (1967), in developing his model of the reading process has also emphasized the importance of predictions for the proficient reader. He suggests that the more the reader can predict, and the fewer the number of cues he requires from the text to confirm those predictions, the better off he is in that reading situation.

Now, a child who speaks English need not be taught to predict. He already has learned to do this when he began to learn to talk. What is necessary however is the following.

First, a child must be shown that, when he attempts to understand written language, he can continue to rely on the predictions he has learned to make in understanding spoken language. He must learn to hone his predictive ability so as to rely on it in a new way.

Second, when reading we make predictions of a different sort than we do when talking or seeing. Writers tend to omit details, for the sake of style, brevity, and interest. A reader must "put the details back" so to speak. The best method of doing this is by prediction. When step A in a plan is mentioned, the reader must predict steps B, C, and D. When D is next mentioned, he must learn to confirm that it has been stated implicitly that B and C have occurred.

An alternate method of doing this is to tie together a chain of events after all the events have been heard. People actually use both methods in understanding. However, the latter method is the clear second choice to be used only when everything else fails. When a reader uses this method, he becomes conscious of trying to "figure things out." Often he can do this, but it takes longer and does not carry with it that feeling that occurs when a prediction is satisfied—of having suspected "that something like that might happen all along."

The process of learning to use predictions to fill in what is implicit, at all levels of knowledge, is fundamentally the most significant part of reading. This forms a large part of what must be taught in teaching reading.

TEACHING A CHILD TO PREDICT

The first formal "reading" instruction a child receives should exploit what he knows about spoken language and orient him towards written language. Since a child can make many reliable predictions in matters he understands, what we want to do when we start to teach him to read is to get him to feel confident about what word in a sentence is likely to come next on the page. It is easier to "read" a word that you have good reason to believe is there. That is, context helps a great deal.

The simplest predictions that one can make in reading are what word will come next in a story one has heard over and over again. Thus, one might begin by reading the story over and over again. After the children have come to really "know" the story, we can initiate the teaching of prediction by leaving out the last content word in a major paragraph. Thus you might say:

Johnny went to the store.
At the store he bought a _____.

Simply stop after "a" and pause. The first time you do this, the children in the class may be a little confused as to what is expected of them. Eventually however, they will enjoy the game of saying out loud the word that has been left out. The important point here is to leave out a content word that appears at the end of a sentence. The omitted word should be of major significance to the story. Children do not easily forget that Johnny bought a "rabbit" or a "top" or whatever. Do not try leaving out words such as "now," "yesterday," or "after" (as in "happily ever after") at first.

An interesting variation on this word-omission method is the word-substitution method. Try substituting for the word to be predicted a silly word, or a word with similar content but different meaning. (For example, say "bear" for "rabbit" or "boy" for "girl"). Most children find this to be great fun if it is done in a jocular way. Allowing them to "correct you" achieves the same purpose as word omission.

After the children have learned to predict the words that come in a story, we can begin to give them the opportunity to identify the written words that correspond to those they have predicted.

Use large charts that have the story printed on them, and put your finger under each word as you read. Your finger should be under the omitted word when the children are being asked to recall it. The actual orthographic shape of that word—what it looks like on the page—will, with very little effort at all, begin to be associated with the word.

After a while, the children will have begun to memorize the story. You can exploit this memorization by having the children go up to the chart you have been using and "read" it to you by having each child place his finger under each word as he says it.

By doing this, you are familiarizing him with the process of reading and beginning to implant in him the idea that one group of letters indicates one word. Of course, this is not the only way to teach the idea that words can have a written form. It is however, an easy one that can be used very early on in the child's schooling. Furthermore, it teaches the important ideas that:

1. symbols can mean words
2. one's expectations are worth relying upon

A child needs to fully understand these ideas, to be ready to read.

The next step in learning to read is learning to associate sounds with words. In order to associate a meaning with a written word, the child must learn to recognize the symbol on the page as a combination of sounds with which he is already familiar. Thus the teaching of symbol-sound associations is the crucial next step.

WORD RECOGNITION

Of course, it is difficult to know when your prediction is accurate if you cannot recognize the orthographic shape of a word. The next step in reading, therefore, is to learn how to recognize a word.

A great deal of discussion among people who are concerned with teaching reading involves the issue of whether a child should be taught to read by use of "phonics" or by "sight reading." Such arguments seem to me to be, for the most part, irrelevant. To see why I say this, see what method you, as an adult reader, use. If you use only sight you might have trouble pronouncing (or "reading") this word:

misdemeanant

If you think you read only by phonics try:

Greenwich, Connecticut

Obviously adults use both sight reading and phonics. Considering that both methods are used, the next question is which one is used first and which second?

Here again the answer seems plain enough. If we used phonics first, we would initially fail at reading "Greenwich, Connecticut" if we try to sound it out, and we would then recall that we knew it all along by sight. Clearly this is not what happens. Rather, after we fail to recognize something by sight, we resort to "sounding it out."

So the normal method of adult reading is to attempt first to recognize a word in one lump, by sight, and if that is not possible, to attempt to piece out of its sound by what we know of the spelling and pronunciation rules of English. To proceed in this manner, however, requires that we have a stock vocabulary of words that we recognize by sight. Ideally, this "sight-recognition vocabulary" should be nearly identical with the our "speech-recognition vocabulary." That is, we should be able to "sight read" nearly every word we know.

In the end a great deal of reading fluency comes down to this issue. The more facility one has at recognizing words by sight, the faster and easier one can read. But such a recognition vocabulary is clearly not inborn; it must be acquired. The question is "how?"

The answer, with respect to children, is to teach them principles they can use in reading all through their lives. First, attempt to recognize something by sight, and if you cannot, sound it out until it sounds like something you do recognize. (Frequently, for beginning readers, such recognition occurs in the middle of the process of sounding out a word.) Initially, of course, the child will be attempting to sound out words that he cannot immediately recognize by sight. But, he will be gradually shifting over to the point where sight-reading predominates. A sight reading vocabulary is built up by reading. Words recognized initially by phonics, after enough repetition, are eventually recognized by sight. Words with irregular spelling should be taught by sight right from the start.

FAMILIAR SIGNS

One way to begin the process of teaching reading by sight is to make use of the sight-reading capabilities that the average child in kindergarten already possesses.

Most six year olds in the United States know all about Burger King, stop signs, and Mobil Stations for example. Each of these is a unique symbol. Common symbols, with words written on them, are easy for a child to recognize. It is a short step from the recognition of a word that is part of a common symbol to the recognition of that word in the absence of its symbol.

What I shall call the "sign game" proceeds as follows. Obtain some pictures of everyday street scenes that contain standard-shaped signs with writing on them. Examples of this include stop signs, exit signs, WALK and DON'T WALK, and various commercial signs. Have the children identify these signs. Most of them probably can do so.

The next step is to write on the blackboard the words that appear on the signs, in letters similar in style to those of the sign. At first, children may have difficulty making the transition to "reading" what you have written. After all, they are not "reading" the words on the sign but are simply recognizing the entire sign—colors, shape, letters and all. But words like STOP and EXIT, can be easily disconnected from their backgrounds. Soon the child will be "reading by sight." If you have simultaneously been using the previously mentioned prediction method, this too will seem to be another verification of the child's ability to predict words. We are now ready for the next step.

THE ALPHABET

As I have said, reading cannot proceed by sight recognition alone, certainly not at the early stages. The next step is to teach the fundamentals of sounding out words. This requires knowledge of the alphabet, however, so it is now time to teach the alphabet.

Many children know the alphabet before they enter school. Unfortunately, what the child has learned from memorizing the alphabet is only partially useful. Becoming accustomed to the shape of the letters of the alphabet is of great value, but the child will probably also have learned the names of the letters. Letter names are entirely superfluous to learning how to read. To see this point, try to recite the alphabet in a foreign language you speak less than fluently. This can be a rather difficult task. The names of letters in a language are almost entirely useless (except in telephone numbers that use letters and the like, or in spelling something for somebody). It can't hurt to know them, of course, but their relevance for reading is nil.

So, your first task in teaching the alphabet will be to teach it again—this time, so it will be more useful to the child. The consonants should be taught with the following new names:

B	"buh"
C	"sss" or "kuh"
D	"duh"
F	"fff"
G	"guh"
H	"h" (just an h and a puff of breath)
J	"jeh"
K	"kuh"
L	"ll"
M	"muh"
N	"nuh"
P	"puh"
QU	"kwuh"
R	"rrr"
S	"sss"
T	"tuh"
V	"vuh"
W	"wuh"
X	"eks" (the name actually works here)
Y	"yuh"
Z	"zzz"

Basically, the idea is to make the sound of the letter with as little extra noise as possible. This turns out to be difficult to do for certain sounds. So, I am suggesting that you add "uh" or "eh" to these sounds, but attempt to make this part as small a sound as possible. That is, "duh" is not pronounced at the stereotypical dunce's sound; it is much shorter than that.

The vowels in English are very complicated, of course. To start, just teach the simplest vowel sounds:

A   "aaa" as in hat or cat
E   "eh" as in bed or ten
I   "ih" as in tin or hip
O   "ah" as in hot or pop
U   "uh" as in but or fun

There are a great many different ways to pronounce each of the letters that represent vowel sounds in English. This will really not bother the child. The reason is simple. As noted before, spoken English precedes written English (both developmentally and historically). The child already knows how to pronounce these words. Of course, he will make initial mistakes in pronouncing irregularly spelled words, but since he is reading only words he already knows and is shifting over to sight reading on his own, these words should present no problem after the first few encounters. He can learn exceptions and will be constantly doing so in his normal learning of the tenses and conjugations of English. The exceptions will not bother him much. Once he memorizes the words as part of his sight recognition vocabulary he will not even notice the discrepancies. Notice for example that the letter "o" in the following words is pronounced differently each time:

phone
you
words
pronounced
not
bother
for

It is actually difficult to notice such things unless they are brought to your attention.

MANIPULATING LETTERS

Once a child has mastered the sounds associated with each letter he is ready to start manipulating letters. This can be done while teaching the alphabet. It is necessary to have on hand a set of large letters that are manipulable by a child. Allow the children to get used to playing with the new letters as if they were toys.

Now let me say a few things about language. We usually group the sounds of a language into consonants and vowels. The simplest unit of speech is what is known as the CVC cluster, a unit of sound that starts with a consonant, is mediated by a vowel, and ends with a consonant. CVC clusters are often what is referred to when people discuss syllables. But remember that just because linguists find distinctions such as CVC clusters, syllables, consonants, and vowels of use in describing language, this does not mean that such notions need or ought to be taught to children. As I have said, they already "know" them in the only sense of know that will ever have relevance to them (unless, of course, they become linguists). The extent to which the notion of a vowel should be taught is that the five vowels should be placed in a separate pile from the consonants. When the child manipulates the letters he should be taught to make CVC clusters.

To start teaching reading, one has to identify the CVC clusters that are words that the child already knows, and that are spelled in a regular (i.e., non-peculiar) way. The idea here is the same as will be used throughout this book. We rely upon the knowledge the child already has in order to teach him to read about what he already knows.

Some words that meet the criteria that I suggest are:

RAT   PAT   HAT   CAT   MAT   SAT   FAT

Any child knows these words. Now the trick is for him to read them.

Actually this is done quite easily. Take the letters A and T, put them together, say "at," and then have the child say it a few times. Now take the R, P, H, C, M, S, and F and, one by one, place them in front of the AT. Say the word that is now made by the new addition, or - and this frequently works well if the child has really learned the sounds associated with the letters - put the letter in front of the AT and have the child attempt to figure out the word.

Some of the potential words that can be used in the manipulation game are shown in Table 1.

Clearly, some letter combinations are better than others. I have not included in this list some CVC's that make words. The words I have left out are either not in a six year old's vocabulary or are ones where the

TABLE 1

	B	C	D	F	G	H	J	K	L
AT	BAT	CAT		FAT		HAT			
IT	BIT			FIT		HIT			LIT
ET					GET		JET		LET
OT					GOT	HOT			LOT
UT	BUT	CUT							
AN		CAN		FAN					
EN			DEN			HEN			
AD	BAD		DAD			HAD			
ID			DID			HID			LID
ED	BED			FED					LED
AP		CAP							LAP
OP						HOP			

	M	N	P	R	S	T	V	W
AT	MAT		PAT	RAT	SAT			
IT			PIT		SIT			
ET	MET	NET	PET					WET
OT		NOT	POT					
UT		NUT						
AN	MAN		PAN	RAN		TAN	VAN	
EN	MEN		PEN			TEN		
AD	MAD		PAD					
ID				RID				
ED				RED				
AP	MAP	NAP						
OP	MOP					TOP		

correct pronunciation (e.g., put) is not in accord with the English orthography.

There are, of course, many more combinations that are possible. Children enjoy reading nonsense words as well as real ones. there is no harm in letting them do this if you inform them that such CVC's are not real words. It is important that they understand when they are reading real words.

PUTTING IT ALL TOGETHER

A child who can identify three letter words (CVC's) correctly and can accurately predict a large number of the words in stories he knows (i.e., that he has memorized), is ready to read.

The first step in combining his powers of prediction and recognition is to induce him to read the words you have been leaving out of stories. This is not as easy as it sounds. After all, he already knows what word has been left out. He need do no more than say the word. You really will not be able to tell if he is reading it or not. But it doesn't matter that much since the child will feel that he is reading, and that is quite important.

Ask him to read aloud, pointing to each word. At first he will go much too quickly for his finger. Make him slow down and coordinate what he says with where his finger is. The point is to convey gradually to the child the feeling of being able to read whole sentences or paragraphs (or even an entire book!).

Gradually the child will actually read the words. That is, since he knows what words are there, and he knows something of how to recognize a word, he will begin to recognize new words that he knows have to be there. It is here that it is possible to help him along.

Begin by helping the child to find the words in a book with which he is very familiar and that are the same as the CVC's he has already learned to read. There should be at least a few of them in any simple story.

Simply point out every "man" or "get" in the book. Then find one and ask him to read it. This is very important. There is a considerable difference between the manipulable letters the child has been playing with and the physical appearance of letters on a page. Beyond size, you may have been using capitals exclusively for manipulation, while most texts are written in lower case and upper case.

Until this point, it is best not to have been too concerned with lower case letters. They represent just one more source of confusion in reading. Introduce lower case letters after reading has begun so that, rather than being a serious source of confusion, they will be just a bit of a bother in a world where the child is *already* confident.

Point out, one by one as needed, the small a's from the big A's, the small b's from the big B's, and so on. Starting with words that use the letters c, f, j, k, m, o, p, s, u, v, w, x, and z will help here as these letters bear the greatest similarity to their upper case counterparts. Unfortunately, words like "sop " and "vow" are hard to find and unknown to the child.

When this hurdle is cleared (in a case-by-case manner as I have said— do not try and teach lower case letters all at once), again ask him to read some of the words he knows. Ask the child to find them and point them out to you. Words like "I" and "me" are easy as they appear frequently and are easy to recognize.

Introduce new words that he has not seen before and ask him to find them. Again use his favorite book so he won't be on unfamiliar ground. When he can do this, he will have passed a very significant stage. He will really understand that letters on a page can mean words that he believes to be there. Thus, he can find them himself and begin to read! The new words chosen should be regularly spelled ones. Irregularities ought to be ignored as much as possible in the early stages.

SYNTACTIC/SEMANTIC PREDICTION

As I said earlier, the key to reading and understanding is our ability to predict what will come next. I have discussed the process of accustoming a child to trusting his predictions when those predictions are based on pure memorization. Of course, memorization-based predictions are the least useful in life. We rarely encounter experiences that we have memorized that need to be processed again. So, the next step in learning to rely on predictions is to expand the scope of the predictions. This can be done by the "sentence game."

Make some large squares of cardboard or paper, and write some words on these squares. You need not use exactly the words I suggest, but these work well:

(1)	(2)	(3)	(4)	(5)
THE	MAN	SAW	THE	CAT
THIS	BOY	ATE	THIS	DOG
A	GIRL	HIT	A	PIG
THAT	CAT	BIT	THAT	RAT
	DOG	HAD		BAT
	RAT	MET		NUT
		LED		
		FED		

Divide the words into five groups, as shown. Put the pile number on each card, or use different colors for each pile.

The game is simple. Construct a five word sentence, with fixed syntax, out of the words on the cards. A sentence is always of the form 1 2 3 4 5. First you construct a sentence for the child and read it to him. Do this a few times.

Since there are only a few cards, and the child is now used to memorizing (i.e., reading by sight) three-letter words, it will only take a short time to learn to recognize each word by sight. At that point (or earlier if the child prefers) allow the child to construct sentences from the piles and read them to you.

You may have some trouble teaching him to read the words THAT, THIS, and THE. The TH combination is difficult for many children to understand. It is the first spelling irregularity he will have seen. Nonetheless, he will have to deal with it sometime, and this is a good time to start. Patiently go over and over those three words until the child recognizes them. He should get the idea quickly because these three words will always be in the same position in the sentence. Do not concern yourself terribly if he confuses them or fails to generalize the TH when it is met eleswhere. One of the problems in teaching reading is the horrendous rules (or lack of them) for spelling in English. There is little we can do about that except to advocate spelling reform.

THE RATIONALE FOR THE SENTENCE GAME

As I have said, predictive processes are at the root of our understanding. The sentence game helps the child learn to rely on his semantic and syntactic predictions. He already has learned to use such predictions in his understanding and production of speech. We want him to use the predictions he has been using all along in the reading process. At this point, it might be helpful to quickly look at how syntactic and semantic predictions work in understanding.

What is the actual role of a grammar in understanding? Grammars have been proposed as formal descriptive devices, useful for noting formal properties of a language. There is no evidence at all, however, that people actually use grammars (i.e., formal encodings of rules of syntax) in the process of understanding. Grammars do not describe how people *use* language. Rather, they describe the formal relationships that obtain when language is looked at as a mathematical system.

Grammar is often taught as if explicit knowledge of it is relevant in reading. No evidence exists to support that premise.

In our computer program, we use a mixture of predictions to help in understanding. These predictions come from every available knowledge source. One of these sources is syntactic knowledge of the language, but it is only one.

To see how people use predictions in language and to appreciate the range of possible sources, consider the processing of the following sentences:

1. John saw the Grand Canyon flying to New York.
2. The old man's glasses were filled with sherry.
3. John's can of beans is edible.

Each of these sentences in some way "tricks" the person attempting to understand it. Such tricks are valuable for indicating to us what we are doing when we are processing language. In (1), a reader "sees" the Grand Canyon flying and then rejects this as an impossible interpretation. If we relied upon syntactic knowledge first, then we would never get the wrong reading for (1) since the wrong reading is the least preferred of the syntactic choices according to any grammar. Our knowledge of how to process sentences by combining concepts forces us to try to combine "Grand Canyon" and "flying." It is our world knowledge, of course, that ultimately rejects this possibility. A full grammatical analysis of this sentence is never even attempted, much less achieved. In (2), our world knowledge predicts that "the old man" wears glasses and thus the "spectacles" sense of "glasses" is chosen during processing. This prediction is rejected when the actual sentence forces us to fill these glasses with sherry.

In (3), if we used our syntactic knowledge autonomously, we would be forced to note that we had predicted that the "can" would be "edible" and then had rejected that in favor of the "beans" being edible. But the hearers of (3) report no such rejection. They actually fail to notice the syntactic irregularity of (3) (it does say that the can was edible) because their semantic rule that insists that edibility be assigned to whatever edible object is around overrides any syntactic choices they may have had.

As a fourth example, consider processing the following:

An armed gunman took two women hostage today and demanded . . . .

I have interrupted this sentence in the middle to indicate how many different predictions you can have in the middle of a sentence, and what the nature of these predictions can be. We expect that the gunman will ask for money or some transport away from where he is, or else make some political demand. We do not wait to the end of this sentence to process it. Syntactically we expect a phrase here (perhaps the word "that" will introduce the phrase), but such a prediction is at a very low level and is of very little interest compared to the knowledge-based prediction.

From the point of view of reading then, the issue is this. To what extent can we get a child to rely on the predictions that he is comfortable in making when understanding spoken language to help him in understanding written language?

One way to do this is to emphasize his right to make predictions. In the early years this can take the form of asking questions about a story. These questions should not rely on what was literally in the story, but rather should be about what was implicitly in the story. "How did the character feel?" "What would you have done in that situation?" "What do you think will happen next?"

The idea of assessing what will happen next is very important in reading. But here I am using a much broader conception of what will happen next than just the next event. Questions such as what will happen next syntactically, semantically, inferentially, attitudinally, and so on, are all legitimate questions. However, I do not recommend that such questions be raised with children or that they be made to answer them explicitly. A child does not have, and need not acquire, the vocabulary of linguists in order to read.

The sentence game is one way to ask and answer such questions syntactically. Getting the new reader to rely on his expectations at all levels is what reading is all about. Games or questions that exploit and develop this ability are crucial to teaching reading. But recall my caveat once again. It is the skills needed to play these games and answer these questions that are needed. We should not be teaching children a special vocabulary to answer the questions. Learning formal syntactic rules is both difficult and irrelevant. Predictive rules that talk about the *kind* of word that is likely to come next are not. By "kind" I do not mean part of speech. Terms such as "noun" are ill-defined and undefinable. No evidence exists that people have such conceptions in their heads. Is love a noun? Is honesty? Transport? They are all nouns sometimes, but at other times are not. Children can express the kind of word that will come next in more meaningful terminology. They expect a "person," or an "animal," or "someone who does something." Making use of what a child already expects is preferable to teaching him what to expect. It is knowledge of language *use* that is valuable, not knowledge of the formal abstract rules.

THE STAGE IS SET

The stage is now set for formal instruction in reading. The child now knows that letters on a page indicate words; that strings of words appear in sentences; that sentences follow one another to tell stories; and, that reading is fun. Furthermore he has already acquired the ability to sound out a word, to recognize a word by sight, and to predict with a high degree of confidence what word will appear next in a sentence.

The child has also acquired the basic skills associated with reading. Essentially, two major tasks remain in transforming the child's reading ability to that of an adult. First, the child must acquire a large recognition vocabulary. At this stage the child knows only a few words by sight; he must acquire thousands more.

Second, the child must learn to "read." There is an expression in English about "reading between the lines." This use of the word read also occurs in "Do you read me?" Football quarterbacks must "read" defenses. All these uses of read stem from the sense of the term that I am using now. There is a great deal more to reading than simply recognizing the words on the page. Any story, no matter how simple, requires us to fill in unmentioned details, to read between the lines. That is the major obstacle in reading, and that is what the following chapters are about. But, before I discuss this in detail, let me return to the task of expanding the recognition vocabulary.

LEARNING NEW WORDS

When we talk about expanding recognition vocabulary, we are trying to enable the child to recognize words by sight. This would be important in any language, but in English it is crucial. So many words are pronounced differently from how they are written that sounding words out can be very frustrating to a beginning reader. In any case, as we have noticed, sight reading is a natural and basic tool in an adult reader.

Second, and this is the main point, we are not—I repeat, not—trying to teach the child new vocabulary. It is quite common for reading texts to have a major part of their lessons devoted to teaching new vocabulary. This illustrates a lack of understanding of how children learn words. Let me emphasize that children do not learn new words from reading them. I will explain this more carefully in Chapters 10 and 11.

ON WITH THE LESSON

All that having been said, the time for official reading lessons is at hand. The point of such lessons is to teach recognition vocabulary. The child should be helped through sets of simple sentences that contain the words he can already recognize and that introduce new words gradually. These lessons should start when the child has finished and mastered all the games that I have set out.

The first step is to present the child with a set of sentences, on a printed page, that correspond with sentences he presumably can already read:

THIS MAN HIT THE RAT

THE CAT ATE THE HAT

A BOY SAW A GIRL

The task now is to lead the child through sentences that he is prepared to read. This will be the first time that the child has had to read brand new sentences. All of our previous exercises have had something fixed, either the vocabulary, the syntax, or the story itself. The idea now is to create new sentences. The child must gain confidence that he can piece together the meaning of a new sentence that is within his sight recognition capability.

We are trying to build up his recognition vocabulary here. Just because the child can figure out a word's sound by sounding it out does not mean that he can recognize that word by sight. But repeated encounters with a word will increase his sight recognition vocabulary. There are a few rules that must be followed with respect to the kinds of sentences that the child is to read:

1. No words should be introduced that are not already in the child's vocabulary.
2. Irregularly spelled or pronounced words should be introduced after regularly spelled ones.
3. New words should always be introduced with a picture next to them if possible. This allows the child to look back at the picture when he forgets what the word is. He thus learns to eliminate the teacher from the teaching cycle (i.e., he doesn't have to ask).
4. Sentences used should remain at the same level of complexity as those shown in the examples above.

When the child has finished a set of lessons of this kind, which gradually increase the difficulty of the vocabulary and the syntax, he will be able to read at the simplest level. That is, he will be able to read aloud sentences on the page. Now the difficult and most important part of teaching reading begins. The child must learn to understand what the words he is saying mean when they are put together in a story. As we shall see, the meaning of a story is more than the meaning of its individual sentences. This is something a child must learn to deal with since it is the critical aspect of what makes reading difficult.

3 Memory and Comprehension

DECOUPLING READING AND LANGUAGE

At this point, the child has been through a series of steps that included:

1. being read to
2. leaving out key words—the prediction game
3. teaching the alphabet sounds
4. playing with letters to form CVC words—the manipulation game
5. the syntax game
6. reading sentences composed of simple words
7. a progression and escalation of the recognition vocabulary

What should be taught next? Or to put this question another way, what is it that differentiates an adult reader from a child who can read simple sentences? What knowledge does an adult have, that is relevant for reading, that a child does not?

49

Many current reading texts seem to share a basic misconception about what knowledge is relevant for reading. They frequently lump together reading and "language arts." By "language arts" they usually mean a number of things, including the following:

1. the use of dictionaries
2. punctuation
3. prefixes and suffixes
4. compound words
5. reading with expression
6. using an index
7. reading a diagram
8. synonyms and antonyms
9. making an outline
10. spelling
11. syllabification
12. capitalization
13. rules of grammar

All these items may be dealt with in the context of teaching reading, and there are more not enumerated. Although I make no argument that these things should be taught in the schools—indeed, they should be—there is a vast difference between teaching them and teaching reading. It seems that there are two questions worth addressing here:

1. Do these thirteen items have anything to do with reading?
2. Is learning to read adversely affected by coupling "language arts" with reading?

None of the above items have anything directly to do with reading. Some of them are clearly new skills (for example, using an index, using a dictionary, making an outline). But these new skills are unrelated to reading *per se*, and should be dissociated from the teaching of reading. Many people read very well but have little or no familiarity with indices or outlines. Coupling these skills with the teaching of reading can make reading itself seem dull or, even worse, difficult. Since advancing in reading is often tied to advancing through workbooks that couple these skills, a child who reads well can get bored and irritated with "learning to read." (We will return to these some of the problems in teaching some of these specific skills in Chapter 10.)

In order to see why the teaching reading and "language arts"must be decoupled, we must consider the distinction between recognition memory and recall memory. This distinction is crucial for understanding what we are doing when we teach reading.

RECOGNITION VERSUS RECALL MEMORY

People exhibit two distinct memory capabilities. They can recognize an object (i.e., know what it is when they see it), and they can recall some information when they need that information. On the surface, these abilities seem to be merely two aspects of the same thing—memory—as they are, but they are actually quite different. Some examples of the differences between recognition and recall are:

1. We can recognize somebody we know when we see them, but often it is difficult to conjure up their image (i.e., recall their image) in our minds when they are not present.
2. We can recognize the capital of Norway, say, when we see it in a list of three on a multiple choice test, but we cannot recall it without those choices before us.
3. We can find our way to a place we have been only once or twice, by recognizing various clues on the way (following our noses). After we turn right at a certain corner, we are sure that was the right thing to do, but we could never have recalled the name of that street or the identifying landmarks well enough to tell someone else how to get there.
4. We can meet somebody we know and forget their names or what they do, yet we certainly recognize them.

All of these and more are experiences common to everyone, because of this "division" in our memories. This division is not a literal one. It is not as if there were two different memory boxes that contained the information we need. Rather, we are relying upon two different processes for retrieving information from memory.

To see this, imagine that you are the director of a large museum with 5,000 rooms, each containing 100 objects of art. As director you might have some difficulty specifying exactly where in the museum the "blue and white Ming vase with butterflies on it" is located. You might be able to give me a good idea about where I'd be most likely to find it, and where to start looking. Also, you might be able to take me there yourself, making an almost direct path to it. But, 500,000 items are just too many for any person to know off hand the exact location of each. On the other hand, if I put you in the correct room, you would have no trouble identifying it as the correct room without actually having to see the vase itself.

Here again we have the difference between recognition and recall. It is difficult to recall 500,000 items, but it is not difficult to find the specialized knowledge that you have to help you recognize one of those items.

Human memory is very much like the museum mentioned above. Searching it in a thorough manner is actually much more difficult than searching a museum. At least in a museum there is a known organization of the material in it. Some people are better organized than others, and they would be better at recall than others. Recognition, on the other hand, is more directly correlated with knowledge. The more you know, the more you can recognize.

MEMORY AND READING

Now let us return to the teaching of reading. How are these two types of memory-retrieval processes related to reading? Although we shall pay greater attention to the above list of skills in Chapter 10, it is worth discussing some of them here as an illustration of the difference between recall and recognition memory.

Spelling is an example of recall memory. When my daughter was five, she hung a sign on her door that read:

Nobode Alaud

My daughter could read extremely well at five. However, as noted, recognition and recall are very different processes. Reading is a recognition process; spelling a recall process. To read we must recognize each word. To do this we must rely on our prior knowledge to help us. In other words, having seen a word before it is easier to recognize it. We do not need to use recall in the process of word recognition. Spelling, as I just said, is a recall process. To spell, we must find the correct spelling in memory. Thus my daughter could write "NOBODE" by sounding out in her mind "nobody" and writing letters for sounds. Naturally she wrote E for the sound that that letter makes. But, if she had been asked to read what she wrote, she might have said "no bode," since she well knew the rules for word recognition in the sounding out of new words.

Despite the fact that spelling and reading rely on totally different memory processes, they are often coupled in reading workbooks and school curricula. But the ability to read really does not depend upon the ability to spell. (There are many eminent professors who can hardly spell, but no one doubts their ability to read! In some school systems, such professors would have a difficult time being promoted from the third grade.)

Capitalization and punctuation are two skills, certainly quite valuable ones, that relate to the distinction between recognition and recall. Capitalization and punctuation are taught to children as recall phenomena, even though they by now know how to treat them as recognition phenomena. That is, a child can *read* a punctuated text, i.e., recognize it, without necessarily being able to punctuate a text. Actually, learning to punctuate correctly is very difficult, even for adults. It should be taught as a subject in school but, as the inability to punctuate does not affect one's reading ability, punctuation must be decoupled from reading. Learning to punctuate is recall phenomena. In fact, all writing is a recall phenomena, so this same argument applies to capitalization. Here again, recall phenomena must be differentiated from reading. Reading is a recognition process.

KNOWING HOW VERSUS KNOWING THAT

To deal with the remaining subjects on the list above, it will be necessary to discuss the distinction between knowledge of how to do something and knowledge about what you are doing.

Perhaps the best way to proceed is by analogy. There are important differences between knowing how to drive a car, knowing how to fix a car, and knowing how to design a car; similarly, with understanding what went on in a football game, being able to play football, and being able to describe the aerodynamics involved when a football is thrown or kicked.

These differences carry over into language directly. We can understand and speak a language, we can edit and correct the language of others, and we can help to create a theory of language.

People are taught to understand much the way they are taught to drive a car. They see someone else do it, they practice themselves with a few pointers, and after they get the feel of it, off they go. You never have to know a thing about how your car runs, either in theory or in practice, to drive it competently (even magnificently). The knowledge that a performer has of his performance ability is usually limited to being able to describe crudely what he is doing. He is rarely aware of what he knows exactly, he just knows how. He may even be able to teach the "how" that he knows, because this can be done by imitation and correction. The theory need never be understood, and indeed if it is understood, will usually in no way help the performance. Great musicians do not usually understand air flows, nor do they have well developed theories of the physics of sound.

With reading it is much the same. Children learn to talk by imitation and correction. To teach reading and writing to a child capable of understanding and talking, it is necessary to give the information pertaining to reading and writing per se that the child does not as yet have. It follows that to teach writing, one must teach about the formation of letters, capitalization, punctuation, and other writing-specific phenomena. (One must obviously teach reading prior to teaching writing, since it is hard to write if you can't read.)

Some children's difficulty in reading comes from a lack of confidence about guessing what is implicit in what they are reading. Teaching children to rely upon their prior knowledge is the crux of what needs to be taught. On the other hand, we do not want to teach children theories about the formal nature of that knowledge.

An excellent illustration of a problem in this regard involves the teaching of grammar. These days instruction in grammar is usually part of a "language arts" curriculum. In our distinction between knowing how and knowing that, it is clear that every child knows how to form a sentence. The most common definition of grammar states that a grammar defines what is in a language. Since every child who speaks English is speaking English sentences, by this definition he can only be speaking grammatical sentences. To put this another way, the child has rules for putting a sentence together that he uses all the time. These rules constitute the "grammar" that he uses.

It is obvious that, prior to entering school, a child who speaks English has no idea what a noun is. But he does know all the rules that he will ever need for knowing how to manipulate nouns. "Noun" is part of the vocabulary of the language theorist, not the language user.

If grammatical rules in no way affect reading ability, what do they relate to? From a stylistic point of view, they relate to writing, but they only do so at a very advanced stage. To see what I mean, consider the rule "do not use a preposition to end a sentence." In the first sentence of this paragraph, I violated that rule. Actually, since English speakers regularly violate that rule, it is quite clear that it is not a grammatical rule of English. Nevertheless, it is considered poor style.

Making children aware of such rules is important, if they might need to know them. It is important to learn to write well. But writing well is something that must be learned considerably after one learns to read. Teaching grammatical notions to elementary school children is simply premature. Furthermore, that kind of teaching may turn children off to school entirely.

With respect to grammar then, a child who has never heard of nouns and verbs will be in no way handicapped. He will be able to read, and speak, with the best. We do not want to teach a child who already knows *how* to use language, to know *that* he is using certain items, particularly when, far from being like physics, theories of language are at this point in a muddle. No theory has been shown to be correct as of this writing. Why teach children aspects of a theory of syntax that have never been proven and are in no way relevant to the development of skills that they will need?

The important point is that we must teach children those things that will help them in reading. Not everything that is currently part of the reading curriculum has relevance in aiding reading. A great many things that are currently taught are holdovers from outdated conceptions of the three R's. We most certainly do wish to make our children facile with language. But, to do this requires that we first ensure that they are good readers. Teaching reading is not the same as teaching language. A child need not "know that" in order to "know how."

WHAT CAN GO WRONG IN COMPREHENSION

What do we want to teach then? The major issue in teaching reading is comprehension. To read is to understand, after all. Work in Artificial Intelligence has taught us a great deal about understanding. Because of that work, we now have a new view of how to teach comprehension.

Before proceeding, let us assess where we are. At this point, our developing reader has mastered sounding out a word and has acquired a small but useful recognition vocabulary. He knows how to read in the sense that he can open a book that contains vocabulary items that he knows, and he can pronounce all the words.

This stage of reading can continue for some time. Children can rather easily develop a facility for sounding out or recognizing a great many words, many of which they may not really understand at all. They will seem to be reading, if what one counts as reading is the pronunciation of the words on the page.

But reading is, of course, primarily comprehending. And comprehension is hardly indicated by whether a child can utter a string of words aloud. Try reading a foreign language that uses our alphabet, Italian or Spanish for example. Can you "read" these languages? Since their pronunciations conform well to way those languages are written, it is rather easy for an English speaker to become fairly competent in reading aloud in those languages. But what does this demonstrate? Certainly this ability bears no relationship at all to comprehension. A beginning reader is not unlike the above English speaker who can read Italian aloud. Since an adult will want to comprehend what he is reading, teaching him to read Italian requires teaching him the meaning of the words. An adult can then use what he knows about how to comprehend in general, and begin to read Italian. The child must learn not only the meaning of the words, but also what the reading comprehension process requires. The task in teaching reading at this point, then, is to teach comprehension.

To assess the problem of what to teach in teaching comprehension, we must attempt to determine what is likely to prevent a child from comprehending a given text. Or to put it more positively, what must a child know, beyond the issue of word recognition, in order to read a story?

To answer this question, let us consider an actual example and use it as a guide to the problem. The story I have chosen is from an edition of *Treasure Island* that is described as appropriate for 8- to 14-year-olds. I will take seven passages and attempt to indicate the kind of trouble, and the source of trouble, that a child might have in reading those passages.

1. Awkward Expressions

> I remember . . . . when the brown old seaman *took up his lodgings* at the Admiral Benbow.

One problem children have in reading stories is a lack of familiarity with certain idiomatic usage, or modes of expression. Here the problem is obvious because the expression "took up his lodgings" is an out of date phrase. Here the child may well know, or be able to figure out, what each word is, but he may still be confused.

2. Script Instantiation

... lodgings at *the Admiral Benbow*

Adult readers now realize that the sailor has entered a kind of hotel (or inn, as we are later told). But how do we know that? We know it the same way we know that in "Sam ordered a pizza at Luigi's," "Luigi's" is a restaurant, probably an Italian restaurant. We, as adult readers, know how to instantiate scripts. Script instantiation is a crucial part of reading. It will be discussed in detail in Chapter 6.

3. Plan Assessment

"This is a handy cove" the seaman said to my father, "and a well-placed inn. Do you have much company here?"

Here, an adult reader, in context, will recognize that the seaman has a plan to stay at the inn if it is quiet and secluded enough. We assume he is hiding, or that perhaps something even more sinister is occurring. We await the reason why. But does a child? A child must be taught to look for the plans of the characters he meets. He must learn to question their motives and see the larger picture. This is a very difficult thing for a child to learn. It involves a very new point of view for him. Young children tend to accept the people they meet on face value. They trust everybody. Moreover, they accept the world as it is. They do not see or look for sinister plans or plots.

To some extent, television can be an aid here. Children who watch TV will learn something of plot development and sinister plans. But there is a great difference between processing text and processing pictures. In reading, many more inferences must be made about what characters actually have done. With TV, actions are spelled out in detail. Understanding that a character has a plan is facilitated by watching TV. But inferring the details of his plan is very easy when watching TV because we just watch the plan develop. We see every detail of a character's actions. In reading a story, we assess the plot, but we also must infer the details.

Most plots depict in some way the interaction and blocking of plans and the attempt to achieve goals. Tracking such things in detail is often beyond a child's experience. He must be taught to track plans. This is discussed in more detail in Chapter 8.

4. Background Knowledge of Characters

> Though his clothes and manners were coarse he did not seem to be an ordinary seaman . . . .

Would a child recognize an ordinary seaman from an extraordinary one? What comparison is being made here? Without some knowledge of what a seaman does, looks like, wants, and so on, it is difficult to understand this sentence.

Two things are important here. First, a child should be given stories for which he has the relevant background knowledge. Second, a child must be taught to assess the traits of the characters he meets. What kind of person is being talked about?

5. Plot Development

> One day he took me aside and promised me money if I would keep me eye open for a seafaring man with one leg.

The plot thickens. We know that but how does a child assess this? He must understand something of what a plot is, how stories develop, and so on.

6. World Knowledge

> His stories were what frightened people most of all. Our plain country people were as shocked by his language as they were by the crimes he described. My father believed that the inn would be ruined by the captain's tyranny; that people would stop coming because he sent them shivering to their beds.

To understand this passage, you need to know something of the values and morals of an English town in the eighteenth century. Further, it is most important to know about businesses, inns in particular, and how and why they run. A basic knowledge of commerce is needed here. This story can be understood effectively only in the presence of the appropriate background knowledge.

7. Tracking Props and Goals

"He's a bad one, but there's worse behind him. They're after my sea chest."

This line is the crux of the story so far. It indicates that there will be a fair amount of plot associated with this sea chest. Indeed, the content of the sea chest is the crucial issue in the story. How is the child to know this? How do we know it?

We know it because we know about valuable objects, greed, likely containers for valuable objects, and story structure. When we see a particular prop in a story we expect it to be used in the story. The child must be taught to look out for props and to track the goals associated with those props.

8. Inferences, Beliefs, and Reasoning

When I told my mother all I knew, she agreed we were in a difficult and dangerous position.

Why are they in a difficult position? The story makes it obvious. Our heroes possess objects of value that others know about and will want to steal. But this is not necessarily obvious to a child. A child must be taught to construct chains of reasoning based on beliefs derived from what he has heard so far and from what he knows of life. But what does the child know of life? Some of that kind of knowledge is taught by stories. Much of it must be taught when, or preferable before, a story is encountered. The child must learn to figure out what is going on.

SUMMARY

The key point is that a child must have a well developed sense of the world around him in order to understand stories about the world. This indicates that a great deal of what must be taught to enable reading is not language per se. Rather, it is world knowledge, and the processes that utilize that knowledge, that constitute the key issues in reading comprehension. But how can we teach world knowledge? Should we even try? I will spell out the answers to these questions at the end of this book. It is clear that we can enhance the child's ability to use what he already knows to help him read. This is the main issue in the chapters that follow.

4 Language and Meaning

WHAT'S RELEVANT

If we are to teach what is relevant to comprehension, we need to understand something of language, meaning, world knowledge, and comprehension processes. From this point, we will delve more deeply into the issues that concern the use of world knowledge in comprehension and the relevance of that knowledge in learning to read.

The simplest and most relevant kind of world knowledge available to us when we read is the knowledge we have of the meanings that underlie our language. As we have said, chidren have learned to predict a great deal about what will come next in a sentence in the natural course of learning to speak and comprehend. However, it is not necessary, as we have said, to teach them the principles that underlie their language in order to teach them to read. But, as an aid to reading, they *must* learn to exploit what they already know about their language.

In this chapter, I will discuss some of the fundamental principles that underlie language. It is useful for teachers to understand these principles. This is particularly true in view of the misinformation about language and the importance of syntax that has been so prevalent in recent years.

WORDS

The first question we might ask about language concerns the meaning of words. What does a word mean? To answer that a word means what it says in the dictionary is wide of the mark. Trying to look up the meaning of a word in the dictionary can often be exasperating, due to the circular nature of dictionary definitions. They merely explain words in terms of other words. Surely the mind can't use such a system. How does the mind understand the meaning of a word?

When we speak, we usually find the words we need without thinking about them. However, there are times when we know what we want to say but somehow cannot find the words that best express the idea we have. What we do on those occasions is say in great detail, using many words to express the idea, what we could have said more concisely if only we had been able to come up with the words we were seeking. So, we are left saying "you know, when people talk to each other and really see what the other person means" for "communication," or "the stuff that comes in a can that you spray to kill bugs," for "insecticide."

Which of the alternatives (the longer or the shorter versions) for the encoding of an idea is the one that is actually used by people's internal mental processes when they understand or begin to generate language?

To answer this question it is helpful to examine some simple sentences and their meanings. Consider the sentence: "John upset Mary." One of the first and most important things to realize is that this sentence is ambiguous. That is, we can think of a number of different meanings for this sentence. Consider these three:

John did something to cause Mary to be upset (or anxious).
John knocked Mary over.
John, who should have lost his match with Mary, won.

People rarely think of all the possible meanings for a sentence when they hear one. This is because they hear sentences in context. A sentence is usually preceded by other sentences, or at least certain circumstances, that obviate the alternative meanings that a sentence may have.

Let's return to the first meaning of our sentence (to disturb emotionally). Early in our education, we learned that "upset" is a verb. (Actually, it is also a noun and an adjective.) Since it functions as a verb in our sentence, if we ask the question, "What is the action going on in the sentence?" we might expect that the answer should be "upsetting."

This answer is inadequate if we require that an action be something that an actor do to something else. We can say, "John upset Mary," but we cannot really mean it. That is to say, upsetting is not something one can do to someone. Try and picture John in your mind upsetting Mary. What do you see? Whatever you see (for this sense of "upset") is liable to be quite different from what someone else sees. Because the mental pictures one forms upon hearing a sentence are analogous to what one perceives to be the meaning of a sentence, we can say here that "John upset Mary" has a very imprecise meaning. The meaning of "upset" is quite unclear for the first sense of the word given above. The action denoted by "upset" is unknown. However, the meaning of the rest of the sentence is much clearer. Whatever this unknown action was, we know that the actor of that action was John. Do we know what the object of that action was? The temptation is to say that we do, but the object is quite dependent on the particular action. We do know something about Mary, but not whether she was the object of John's action. For example, Mary may have heard about something John did to someone else, or to himself. Rather, all we know is that Mary was upset (in the sense of anxious) as a result of John's unknown action.

Putting this all together, we have something that we can call the meaning of the first sense of our sentence:

EVENT1: JOHN DID SOMETHING
STATE1: MARY WAS UPSET

RELATIONSHIP: EVENT1 CAUSED STATE1

One of the more important features of the representation of the meaning of the sentence that we have just shown is what it leaves out. We have written that John did something. The fact that we do not know what he did is very important. It points out the imprecision that people use when they speak. We are quite content to leave out the actual action performed by John and speak only about the action's consequence.

This imprecision is not at all unusual. In fact, English has a great many words like "upset." Nearly any word that describes the mental or physical state of a person can be used as a verb or has a verb form equivalent to it. Thus we can have: John killed Mary, John disturbed Mary, John angered Mary, John pleased Mary, and so on.

As understanders we recognize that there has been an action left out of these statements. What do we do about it? The answer is that we often fill in the missing action. The word we use for this is *inference*.

In such sentences there is a great deal of room for misunderstanding. Because we are left to our own devises to guess what John did, we often guess wrong and then forget which part we actually heard and which part we guessed. We may then go on to relate an inaccurate message to the next person we deal with. This is part of the reason that the party game "telephone" can have such unusual outcomes.

Fortunately, the English language does provide help in being more precise. To tell about the action that has been left out we can use a "by" phrase. That is, we can say, "John upset Mary by yelling at her." This informs us of the action that was missing, and we can thus replace the "did something" with "John yelled at Mary" in our present representation.

The rule that we are using here provides an insight into how people actually process sentences. When we hear the "John upset Mary" part of this sentence, we create the representation shown above in our minds. We then use the "did something" as a kind of empty mailbox into which we are prepared to stuff any verb ending in "ing" that follows a "by." Rules such as this are the key to how we understand what we hear. We have an implicit knowledge of rules that tell us where to put "what," and how one thing relates to another in a sentence.

REPRESENTATION OF MEANING

A central feature of language is that two sentences with quite different surface forms can mean the same thing. This fact poses a very interesting question: Is there only one thought in our heads corresponding to these different surface forms? It seems obvious that if there is only one meaning expressed by two different sentences, then there must be only one thought corresponding to it. Evidence indicates that people cannot remember the surface forms of sentences and only remember their meanings (Sachs, 1967; Anderson, 1974). This is not surprising, but it suggests an interesting issue: Which of the two or more possible ways of uttering a particular meaning most closely corresponds to the one used by the mind? That is, is one surface form more basic, more like the thought as it is represented in the mind? If so, which one?

To answer this question we will for the moment pursue another related one. How do we detect similarity in sentences? What makes certain sentences seem to be very close in meaning? To consider this in more detail, let's look at four quite similar sentences:

John gave a book to Mary.
Mary took a book from John.
Mary received a book from John.
Mary bought a book from John.

Each of these sentences shares a common element, but what? It seems clear that some concept denoting a change in the possession of an object is being referred to in each sentence. Is such a concept more basic to the mind than, say, the concept of "buying"? If we consider the elements of language to be analogous to the physical elements, we can see that the answer must be "yes." Just as the physical elements combine to form compounds, the basic mental elements combine to form concepts larger than themselves. What we have above is the combination of the basic mental element "transfer of possession" with other elements to form concepts (and later words) such as "buy" and "give."

The search for the elements of meaning that underlie language and the rules involving the manipulation of those meaning elements is thus the key problem in understanding how language functions.

CONCEPTUAL RULES

What kinds of concepts do we use when we understand? How do those concepts combine? Understanders must employ rules that allow them to decide how to combine concepts that are presented to them in a sentence. Sometimes these rules are the grammatical rules of English, but often they are not. For example, a sentence such as "I saw a building walking down the street" is understandable in two possible ways. However, a hearer is much more apt to assume that the speaker was walking down a street and passed a building than that a building was actually walking down the street, because we know rules of the world that tell us which possibility is more likely. As understanders, our job is not to rule out possibilities, rather it is to choose between them. Our preferences, in ambiguous situations are based on what we know about the world.

CONCEPTUAL CATEGORIES

There are different types of concepts, and there are rules for combining these types of concepts to make coherent meaning structures. Let us look at the syntactic categories of English, as a way of considering what the categories of concepts might be like.

A noun is often defined as a person, place, or thing. This is very nice as long as one takes no notice of all the abstract nouns that are available. Words such as "honesty," "transportation," and "hatred" do not fit nicely into all sentences where a noun is needed. To make matters worse, words like "love," "upset," and "desire" are clearly verbs when we first look at them, but sentences such as "The upset of the Vikings was costly for John" or "My desire for you is strong" are common enough. These verbs are quite clearly nouns in such sentences.

Examining these sentences can give us a good idea about the elements that comprise thoughts. If we ask what "desire" means in the above sentence, we cannot help but realize that its meaning there is no different than its meaning in the sentence "I desire you." Noun or verb, the meaning is the same. Of course, it is not easy to put our fingers on exactly what "desire" does mean in either sentence. But it is obvious that, whatever we decide that meaning to be, both the noun and the verb meanings of "desire" will belong to the same conceptual or mental category.

At this point we must ask the question: What kinds of meanings can a word have? One of the most straightforward answers to this question is that, although "noun" may be a rather odd notion, there is a subset of what we call nouns that behave very simply and are therefore a possibly useful category. Certain words (or rather the ideas behind certain words) only have one function in a sentence. This is so for a very good reason. They are things or objects, and cannot be but what they are. Words such as "rock," "butter," "man," and "tree" are examples of these. Yet as soon as we look at these concrete examples, a peculiarity arises which in many ways bears greatly upon our problem of trying to divorce the ideas describing the language of the mind from our knowledge of English. All of these words can also be used as verbs! If this is the case, how are these words any different from the words we have just previously discussed?

If we look closely at these words, however, we can see a very important difference. When they are used as verbs, none of these words mean anything much like what they meant as nouns! Whereas before the words we worked with meant exactly the same thing as nouns or verbs, this new set of words often have very unrelated meanings when they change from nouns to verbs ("John rocked the boat," for example), or only slightly related meanings ("John treed the cat" or "John manned the oars"). What is the significance of this?

The answer is that here we are dealing with concrete objects. It happens that in English many words have come to have multiple meanings. Since a language of the mind is a language that combines and uses meanings rather than words, it is entirely irrelevant if the same sound happens to stand for a number of different meanings. If is, of course, not irrelevant to the understander who must decode this mess, but the mind itself will see these things as entirely different. Whatever the historical reason for the two different meanings of rock (of course there are in fact a great many more), they must be exactly that in the mind—two different conceptual entities or ideas. Mentally, therefore, what is two is actually one (i.e. no matter what the role of "desire" is in the sentence, the meaning of the word is the same) and what is one is actually two (i.e. the word "rock" has at least two, very different meanings.)

We can see then that there is a useful entity in the mind—the concrete object—that will serve as one of the conceptual types we have been seeking. The concrete object is something we can understand and deal with. We can recognize how these objects behave in combination with other mental types (the syntactic combinations of the mind) and we can recognize our experience with dealing with these objects (the semantic combinations of the mind). Thus, concrete object will serve as one possible mental type.

ACTIONS

What other conceptual types exist in the mind? In asking this, we may as well make use of the first type we have found. We can do so by asking the following questions: In what way do concrete objects combine? That is, how do objects function in a mental environment? What do we say about objects, or more precisely, what do we mean about objects when we incorporate them into things we say?

These seem like rather easy questions to answer. Objects have things happen to them. Also, certain objects can themselves do things. This is a simple statement about what we know to be true of the world around us. The key method of combining concepts to make meaningful statements is by the use of actor-action-object constructions. That is, we can define an event as being made up of at least an actor, an action, and an object.

Now in saying this, we must keep in mind that a type of conceptual idea and its function in an event are not the same thing. What we are doing here is not giving more types, but rather beginning to think about the conceptual construction rules (those we have been calling syntactic) that are available to the language of the mind. What we mean by this is that a concrete object (a rock, a tree, a man) can function as a conceptual syntactic object, that is, as a thing to which or on which an action is performed. This distinction between concrete objects and conceptual syntactic objects becomes a bit clearer when we consider actors.

What type of object can be an actor in the real world (and therefore in the means we have available to us for understanding the real world)? Not every concrete object can act. Rocks cannot *do* anything in the world, while on the other hand people and animals certainly can.

Let's examine the consequences of what we have been saying. We have said that actions exist, but we have in no way defined an action. In addition we have said that only animate objects can act. One of the consequences of this last statement is that we have ruled out conceptual constructions that are perfectly permissible in English. For example, "The rock hit the boy" and "The window broke" are quite sensible sentences. Both of these sentences have inanimate subjects (in English) that are concrete objects. To put it another way, what do such sentences really mean?

The answer to such questions depends greatly on what we mean by the idea of an actor and an action. We offer the following definitions: An actor is a concrete object that can decide to act upon some concrete object in some way. An action is what an actor does to a concrete object. By these definitions, a rock can never be an actor because it can never decide to do anything. Similarly "broke" can never be an action, because it is not something that some actor can decide to do. (An actor can perform an action that results in "breaking," but that is another matter.) Since the former of these points is much more obvious than the latter, we shall take it up first.

A sentence such as "The rock hit the boy" is understood very differently from "The man hit the boy." As understanders, we recognize that rocks never really act. What we do when we hear such sentences is to put them into an internal form (the language of the mind) that rectifies the sloppiness of English and makes clear what must have happened. We do not for a minute imagine that the rock decided to do anything. That is, we do not see "The rock hit the boy" as being similar to the sentence "The man hit the boy." Rather we recognize immediately that rocks are inanimate concrete objects, and that inanimate concrete objects ordinarily function as objects of an action. Conceptually, then, the rock in this sentence must be an object of someone or something else's action. "What role does the boy play?" and "Who is the actor?" are two important questions to ask here. As understanders we must also concern ourselves with determining what the action in this event is. Let us think about this event a bit. What really must have happened? For a rock to hit a boy certain things must be true. First of all the rock must have been in motion. Also, since rocks cannot put themselves in motion, something must have put the rock in motion. Three choices seem possible: (1) a person or an animal; (2) a natural force, such as the wind, the ocean, or an earthquake; or (3) a machine.

The next question is: "Done what?" We really do not know what action set the rock in motion; it could have been pushed, swung, thrown, or whatever. We do know one thing however, the action we are concerned with is not "hit," as found in our sentence. (True, the rock may have been hit to set it in motion, but this is not the same instance of hit. When a rock is set in motion by an actor, a contact between the actor and the rock has taken place. In "The rock hit the boy," it is the rock and the object that are in contact.) To avoid guessing about exactly what action took place, it is more useful not to restrict ourselves to English names for specific actions. Rather we should begin to search for generic action names that incorporate many specific actions into a situational setting. If all we know is that the rock was set in motion, it would be perfectly reasonable to call this action something like "set in motion." However, in order to set something in motion it is necessary to apply a force to it. Thus an even more general name for the action we need is APPLY FORCE. (The difference between these two is simply a difference of one more consequence for "set in motion." APPLY FORCE can include many more types of specific actions than "set in motion," because the latter is only one possible consequence of applying force (imagine pushing the Empire State Building with your hand). Because all "set in motions" are first APPLY FORCEs when applied to inanimate objects, we shall use the simpler term.)

What kind of entity is the action that we are representing with the symbol—APPLY FORCE? It is a simple, basic action, that underlies a great many possible verbs. (We shall explore the consequences of this later on in this chapter.) Most importantly, APPLY FORCE is an action that describes a commonplace occurrence in the world. We shall use its precision and simplicity as we proceed in our discussion of the nature of language processing.

So far our analysis of this sentence then, we have an action—APPLY FORCE; an object—the rock; and one of three possible types of actors— animate, natural, or machine. What happened to the boy? "The boy" is the target or direction of the APPLY FORCE of the rock (and therefore of the rock itself). Thus we have the following event:

```
actor:unknown
action:APPLY FORCE
object:rock
direction:boy
```

We can see, by thinking about the sentence again, that this analysis does not completely express all the information in the sentence. If the rock hit the boy we know that a contact occurred between the rock and the boy. Furthermore, we know that this contact occurred as a result of the APPLY FORCE event described above. Thus we have two objects in contact, which can be expressed as:

```
relationship:contact
    object 1:rock
    object 2:boy
```

What remains is to determine the connection between the event and the relationship (or state of the world). The connection is, of course, simple causation. Thus we can represent the meaning of the sentence "The rock hit the boy" as:

actor:unknown
action:APPLY FORCE
object:rock
direction:boy
  ⬇ CAUSED
relationship:contact
object 1:rock
object 2:boy

What have we accomplished with this kind of representation? First of all, we have begun to examine the meaning of the sentence in a precise, unambiguous format. Languages such as English are, as we have said, highly ambiguous and imprecise. There is no reason at all to believe that the language of the mind is either ambiguous or imprecise, however. People know what they think they have heard (even though it may not correspond to what the speaker wanted them to have understood). People determine what events took place from what they hear. If the sentence they hear is ambiguous, understanders will usually determine one precise meaning for it and then ignore any other possibilities.

Secondly, we have determined what really happened. We have had to decide on the particular meaning of the highly ambiguous word that was used, "hit." In doing so we have had to make explicit all the relationships that exist between the objects and actions in the sentence.

ACTIONS VERSUS STATES

We can now return to our consideration of how actions are performed. We noted in the previous section that when we say "The rock hit" we mean "Something applied a force to the rock causing it to collide with." If this is the case, then what exactly is an action, and how can we recognize and identify one? (Recall that here we are talking about conceptual actions, such as APPLY FORCE, rather than specific verbs, such as "push," "shove," "pull," etc.) We need to explore how people think about actions, or rather how the mind deals with actions.

The second example above was "The window broke." We can see that
this example is a great deal like its predecessor. Here again something
must have applied a force to the window (or applied a force to an object in
the direction of the window). The effect of this action was to cause a new
state of the world to occur—the window passed from an unbroken state to a
broken state. All of this seems obvious enough, but still it seems that we
have begged the central question: What action actually took place? It is
clear that "break" itself is not an action as we have defined actions,
because the word "break" does not tell us about the action that was
performed. It tells us only about the *result* of the action that was
performed. Again, as with the rock and the boy, there are many possible
actions that could have resulted in a broken window. A boy could have
kicked the window; the wind could have blown the window out; a bullet
could have flown through it. We simply do not know, from the sentence
itself, what action took place - "kicked," "hit," "pushed," and "shot" are
only a few possibilities.

What do we know then? It is very important to note that our lack of
information at this point is itself information. The fact that we do not know
what action took place means that we may need to discover it somewhere
else in the understanding process. To do this, we need to know what it is
that we do not know. Since it is not possible to remedy a lack of
information without recognizing that such a lack exists, the very knowledge of the lack is itself useful information. Thus, it is crucial to our
understanding the sentence that we recognize that the actor and the action
in our sentence are both unknown. The representation for "The window
broke" is:

    actor:unknown
    action:unknown
    object:window

       ↓ CAUSED

    state:broken
    object 1:window

A paraphrase for this is: something happened to the window that caused it to break. Our ability to make inferences is then used to determine that the unknown action must be APPLY FORCE.

We still have not solved the problem of delimiting what can and cannot be an action. We now know only that "break" is not one. Let's reiterate why this is so. "Break" is not an action, because it specifies only the state that results from an action. We are not denying that it is a verb, of course, but as we have seen before, such syntactic notions are of dubious value when speaking about problems of meaning. "Break" is not an action because there is no way to know how to do it until it is done. We can plan to break something, of course, but what we do may not succeed. The fact that the action performed did not break the window does not change the action. If I kick a window, the action is still "kicking," whether or not I succeed in breaking the window. The success or failure of the intention of an action does not alter the nature of the action itself. It may alter the verb we choose to use to describe what we did, but it does not alter what we actually did.

To explore further the nature of actions, let's examine a number of other sentences. Consider, for example, "John hurt Mary," "John punished Mary," or "John prevented Mary from leaving town." Here again we must point out that neither "hurt," "punish," or "prevent" are actions. There are many actions that will fit into the unknown action slot in our diagram (that is, the action slot in an actor-action-object construction). To hurt someone, you could hit him, kick him, yell at him, kiss a rival, damage his property, and so on. The problem is made more complex, of course, by the fact that there is more than one kind of "hurt." But no matter what kind of "hurt" we choose to talk about, we are talking about a state that describes the object in the sentence (object as a syntactic notion, not a conceptual one). Thus our representation of "John hurt Mary" must be:

actor:John
action:unknown
object:unknown
   ↓CAUSED
  state:hurt
  object:Mary

The understanding of sentences is driven by our knowledge of what the verbs in those sentences really mean. Once we have established the relationships between the participants in an event, as specified by the meaning of the verb used, the rest is easy. The verb tells us where to find each participant in an event, how to recognize him when we see him, and what the final shape of things must look like. What the verb does, then, is point the way to the blank, unfilled slots in the structure of the event.

It should be clear then that the key to understanding is the knowledge of the nature of events. We must know that events are comprised of actors, actions, objects, and directions, and we must know what objects and relationships in the world can fill what slot. It is the decomposition of verbs into their basic elements that makes this all possible.

PARAPHRASES AND CANONICAL FORMS

One of the key issues in determining how people understand language is the problem of paraphrase. We know from our everyday use of language that is it possible to say the same thing in many different ways. Each of the different ways is simultaneously the same and different. That is, a given meaning can be expressed in ways that show that the speaker is literate, scholarly, or poorly educated, as well as angry, relaxed, or upset, and so on. Events can be expressed in a journalistic style or a novelist's style, in a professional style or a hillbilly's style. But the events, once they are expressed, are the same events, no matter how they have been expressed. Now we are by no means saying that how one expresses oneself makes no difference in the end. Rather, we are saying that there are a number of different kinds of things being expressed in a sentence or group of sentences. The one that we shall focus on here is commonly called the underlying or "real" meaning of the sentence, which we shall refer to as the conceptual content of a sentence. The conceptual content of a sentence is the event or events that are being referred to by a sentence's expression. Style, emotional content of words, and the educational value of certain modes of expression will be ignored in our discussion. Having said all that, we can get back to the problem of paraphrase.

It is still possible, ignoring all stylistic issues, to express the same event in many different ways. People are frequently asked to say "something in their own words." This request seems rather absurd, as it is usually impossible for people to do otherwise. We do not remember the words that people say; we only remember the conceptual content of those words. (If you don't believe this, try turning on the television or radio, listening for five minutes, and trying to repeat what you heard. You may be able to paraphase what you heard, but most of the actual words [though not all] will have been lost.)

This raises a very interesting question. If people remember only conceptual content, not actual words, in what form do they remember the conceptual content? To put it more concretely, given the following four sentences, which is *the one* real form you use to remember the content of what is being said?

John prevented Mary from leaving town by breaking her leg.

John broke Mary's leg so she couldn't leave town.

Mary couldn't leave town because of something John did that resulted in her having a broken leg.

Mary couldn't leave town. John was responsible. He broke her leg.

In attempting to answer the above question, bear in mind the following problems: If you believe that any one of these forms is more basic than any of the others, you will also have to accept that there are consistent rulès for translating the other three forms into the form you have chosen. Consistency is a key here. For example, does "responsible" in the last sentence decompose into something that is also implicit in the other three sentences? If so, what is the form into which it decomposes?

If you believe that none of these forms is more basic than any of the others, then what form is used by the mind? If you believe that they are all equally well remembered, then obviously the mind must contain complicated matching and searching rules to go with each form. For example, suppose you hear the fourth sentence and would like to do the simple and everyday thing of saying: "I've heard that before." How can you know that you have heard it before if you stored the original in the form of the first sentence? How will you know in which form you have stored it?

The answer to this (and to the problem of paraphrase in general) is that there is only one possible method by which the mind reduces what it hears into some basic form, and it is always the same form. This basic form, which is called canonical form, must have the following properties, no matter what it looks like:

1. Any representation in a canonical form must be completely un-ambiguous.
2. Any two sentences, in the same or different languages, that have the same meaning, must have only one possible underlying canonical form.
3. There can be no canonical paraphrases; that is, no two canonical forms can mean the same thing unless they are identical.
4. Sentences that are similar in meaning must have canonical forms that are also similar.

What does this canonical form of the mind look like? Obviously it cannot look like any one of the four sentences given above, because the canonical form must be able to express the meaning of all four of them, as well as all of the other possible ways of saying the same thing.

Since all four sentences can be (and must be) expressed by the same canonical form, there must exist rules that allow the mind to translate or "map" from any one of the sentences into the basic canonical form. Conversely, in order to express a thought in a spoken or natural language, generation rules must exist which allow us to map the canonical form into all the possible ways of expressing that form. However, rules of this type are highly complex, and their specifics are well beyond the scope of this discussion.

SIMILARITY OF EXPRESSION: THE BASIC ACTIONS

The key issue with respect to canonical forms is not the isomorphic nature of the forms for the same meanings, but rather the similarity of the forms for similar meanings. This is the case because, although sentences are not often identical in meaning in their real-world expression, meaning similarities occur all the time. That is, we express our ideas a little differently each time, adding and leaving out details as we deem necessary. People don't always say all that they know; they abbreviate, or sometimes embellish. Thus we need to be able to recognize not only when things are identical, but also when they are similar.

To accomplish this, it is necessary to build a basic set of conceptual elements that can be combined so as to preserve the nuances of the language (Schank 1973, 1975). Thus we will be able to understand the complexity of the conceptual contents referred to, but also recognize the similarities underlying those complexities.

To make this more concrete, let's look at some simple sentences and consider how best to analyze and represent their meanings. Consider the sentences:

1. John gave Mary a book.
2. Mary took a book from John.
3. Mary received a book from John.
4. John sold Mary a book.
5. Mary bought a book from John.
6. Mary traded a cigar to John for a book.

We immediately notice that these sentences share a common element, but it is somewhat difficult to put our finger on what it is. Let's attempt to analyze the meaning of (1) and (2) and note their similarities and differences.

As we have said, all events can be characterized by a common conceptual syntax, namely, the actor-action-object-direction combination. Thus, in attempting to analyze (1), we can begin with the empty event:

```
actor:unknown
action:unknown
object:unknown
direction:unknown
```

Of course all of these roles are not unknown. The actor of (1) is clearly John, and the object is clearly the book. What is the action and its direction? For the moment let us simply say that the action is "give". The most common sense of "give" takes an animate direction. That is, we usually give things to animate objects (usually humans). So for the moment we have as our analysis of (1):

```
actor:John
action:give
object:book
direction:Mary
```

Now let us look at sentence (2). The actor here, of course, is Mary; again, the object is "book," and the direction would seem to be "John". But there is something quite different about direction "from" and direction "towards." If we write the direction simply as "John," we will certainly have lost information.

The problem here is that directions have to have two parts in order to be completely specified. If the direction is "from John" in (2) then it has to be "to somebody else" as well. Similarly, in (1), just because we heard only about the "to Mary" part does not mean there is not a missing "from" part lurking about somewhere to be discovered in the remainder of the sentence, or to be figured out for ourselves. Making the assumption that "take" is the action for (2) then, let us revise our analysis of the direction role to account for what we have said for both (1) and (2). This leaves us:

	(1)			(2)	
actor		John	actor		Mary
action		give	action		take
object		book	object		book
direction	TO	Mary	direction	TO	unknown
	FROM	unknown		FROM	John

Although we had expected our analyses of the meaning of (1) and (2) to look somewhat alike, there really does not seem to be any obvious similarity (other than the object in each is book!). But of course there should be similarities; our intuition tells us so.

Part of the problem here is that we have not really dealt with the meanings of "give" and "take." One way to consider what their meanings might be is to attempt to fill in the blank slots in the direction role for (1) and (2). After all, we can figure out from whom the book was a gift in (1). Clearly, it was "John"! In fact, the meaning of "give" specifies exactly that point. The actor is the same as the starting direction (or donor) of the object. Similarly, we know who now has the book in (2)—Mary. The actor of a "take" is the same as the "to direction" (or recipient) of the object. Now let's look at our diagram with these directions filled in:

	(1)			(2)	
actor		John	actor		Mary
action		give	action		take
object		book	object		book
direction	TO	Mary	direction	TO	Mary
	FROM	John		FROM	John

Our analyses of (1) and (2) are beginning to look a little more alike, but something is still missing. To find it, let's step back a minute and consider the differences between the two sentences. They certainly have different actors. But what else is different? They both involve an event with the same overall consequence. The effect of this event is to transfer possession of a book from John to Mary. The only difference between them is the person focused on as actor in the event.

The solution to our problem then is clear. Instead of talking about actions such as "give" or "take," we should consider the action in these events to be the one most clearly associated with the intention and overall effect of the event, namely, "transfer of possession." Thus our analysis will treat these sentences as having a meaning that differs only with respect to the actors in them, as follows:

(1)

actor		John
action		TRANSFER POSSESSION
object		book
direction	TO	Mary
	FROM	John

(2)

actor		Mary
action		TRANSFER POSSESSION
object		book
direction	TO	Mary
	FROM	John

What do we gain and what do we lose from such an analysis? It is possible, of course, in a bad analysis, to lose information. Has any been lost here? We will be able to translate the concept of TRANSFER POSSESSION, where the actor is associated with a TO direction, into the English expression "give." Similarly, a TRANSFER POSSESSION where the actor is associated with a FROM direction will be translated into the English "take." Thus our analysis has in fact lost nothing. What do we gain then?

First of all, we gain a certain economy. Every time we understand a TRANSFER POSSESSION to have taken place, we can react to this concept with certain kinds of information (called inference rules). If we did not have this one conceptual item, then these rules would have to be duplicated for every verb that contained the meaning element TRANS-FER POSSESSION. This loss of economy would be considerable as it is not just a case of "give" and take," but also of hundreds of other verbs that involve the transfer of possession.

Secondly, we capture the similarity of meaning that is so crucial to our understanding. It can readily be seen we could express the same event by (1) or (2). That is, we can see a book change hands and express it either by

(1) or (2), or for that matter (3). Our perspective is slightly different in each case, and that difference is captured by the reversed actors in the analyses. But the overall meanings are pretty close (as they should be, since we may have the same event). Dispensing with the actual verb used and replacing it with the meaning element (or basic action) underlying it solves this problem.

Does the mind use such a basic action as TRANSFER POSSES-SION? It is rather hard to see how it would function without it. The duplication of information and the subsequent inefficiency of storage would be tremendous, as would the endless rules specifying that a "give" here is the same as a "take" there, or that a "buy" is somewhat like a "give" and a "take," and so on.

To see what we mean by this, consider sentences (4), (5), and (6):

4. John sold Mary a book.
5. Mary bought a book from John.
6. Mary traded a cigar to John for a book.

What is the proper analysis of the meaning of the verb "buy"? It seems obvious that "money" is involved, but how? Using the concept of transfer of possession makes the issue clearer. Obviously there are two transfers of possession taking place. The first involves the book; the second, which is causally related to the first, also involves a TRANSFER POSSESSION. But this time, the participant roles are switched and money is the object. The analysis of (5) then is:

    actor:Mary
    action:TRANSFER POSSESSION
    object:money
direction TO:John
    FROM:Mary
    ↑ CAUSED ↓
    actor:John
    action:TRANSFER POSSESSION
    object:book
direction TO:Mary
    FROM:John

(The double arrow here indicates that the two events caused each other.) What is the analysis of (5) then? It seems obvious that since the meaning of (4) is identical to the meaning of (5), their analyses will be the same. (There are some people who see the meaning of these sentences as slightly different, of course. This problem arises from taking sentences out of context, as there are contexts that radically alter the meaning of sentences. Nonetheless, the events referred to are the same in both sentences. In trying to imagine a typical case, out of context, we can get ourselves into trouble. The point is that "buy" and "sell" refer to the same event. Sometimes one word is used instead of another for reasons other than context. "Buy," for example, means the same as "acquire financially," but the latter is pretentious. Nonetheless, the same basic money element of TRANSFER POSSESSION is present in either case.)

Perhaps the most important case to look at in arguing for a basic action such as TRANSFER POSSESSION is sentence (6). Sentence (6) seems a lot like (4) and (5) in meaning, yet there is a considerable difference in the structure of the sentences. This is because "money" is implicit in (4) and (5). Our memory has to fill in "money" in the appropriate place, when it is not specified in the sentence. But in (6), the objects of both TRANSFER POSSESSIONS are specified, and "money" is not involved. The meaning analysis of (6) is identical to that of (5), with "cigar" replacing "money." We know this because the "for" that follows "traded" acts as a cue and tells us the object of the second TRANSFER POSSESSION. What then does TRANSFER POSSESSION do for us? It makes obvious similarities obvious. Since people easily recognize that (5) and (6) are similar, the mind's method of representing this similarity must make use of such basic actions as TRANSFER POSSESSION.

OTHER BASIC ACTIONS

So far we have introduced two basic actions—TRANSFER POSSESSION and APPLY FORCE—that qualify as actions in our conceptual system. It is possible, using the methods and requirements that we have described here, to specify exactly what basic actions will work to represent the physical and mental worlds about which we commonly speak. But, again, this is beyond the scope of this book. I shall just briefly summarize the results of our research on the representation of actions, and thus the representation of meaning, in what follows.

A very important basic action is TRANSFER INFORMATION (which we shall abbreviate here as T.I.). There are hundreds of verbs whose main meaning element is T.I. Some of them are: "read," "tell," "see," "hear," "remember," "forget," "teach," "suggest," "promise," and so on. The important thing about each of these verbs is that they all transfer information, not incidentally, but as their main focus. This is not to say, of course, that these verbs mean the same things. Clearly they do not, but they do share a very significant part of their meaning. Their differences are no less significant. Any meaning representation must account for both their similarities and their differences. For the purpose of showing how meaning analysis works when using basic actions, let us consider the verbs: "read," "tell," "see," and "promise."

First, we note that both "see" and "read," are close to each other in meaning, as are "tell" and "promise." That is, although all four verbs have the common element of T.I., the analyses we expect to find for "see" and "read" should be quite similar, as should be the ones for "tell" and "promise."

To "see" is to TRANSFER INFORMATION from one's eyes to one's mind. To "read" is to TRANSFER INFORMATION to one's mind by focusing one's eyes on a book. So, we need to represent two new things in order to analyze "see" and "read." First, we need some representation for our own minds, that is, for our conscious processing capabilities. (Bear in mind here that we do not need a psychologist's explanation of how the brain works; we are simply trying to represent how people think. Therefore, we only need represent what a naive person thinks about when he hears a sentence containing the word "see" or "read".) Secondly, we need to represent the instrumental action of focusing the eyes.

"Tell" and "promise" are also quite similar. "Tell" is the transfer of information between people by means of speech. "Promise" implies that information about a future event has been transferred. The important point is that these verbs, and thus sentences containing them, have key meaning elements in common. Understanding must involve decoding verbs into these key basic elements, so that we can draw the correct inferences from what we hear. For example, a key inference from T.I. is that the hearer in each case now knows some new information that was once in the mind of the speaker. This is true whenever T.I. is used, regardless of the verb used to express it.

It should be clear that since actions such as T.I. and TRANSFER POSSESSION form the basis of so many verbs, the number of basic actions is actually quite small. So far, we have presented the actions:

TRANSFER INFORMATION
TRANSFER POSSESSION
APPLY FORCE

Actually only three more basic actions make up the elements used in the vast majority of actions that we commonly talk about. These are:

TRANSFER LOCATION
INGEST
CONCLUDE

To illustrate how these last actions are used, consider these sentences:

John went to New York.
John took a plane to New York.
John drank some milk.
John decided to go home.

"Going" is simply transfer of location. However, we have required that all events have certain parts, and it will be noticed here that there is no obvious candidate for the conceptual object. That is, what was transferred? The answer is that since we are prone to speak of self-locomotion, the verb "go" does not take a syntactic object. All actions have a conceptual object, however, so although it seems quite funny to say "John walked himself to the store," conceptually this is just what we do mean.

Thus the conceptual actor for "go" is usually the same as its conceptual object.

The second sentence is a bit deceptive on the surface. The verb is "take." We might imagine, if we were extremely naive, that since "take" was used before to mean TRANSFER POSSESSION, that this is the meaing element involved here. However, consider the following sentences that use "take":

John took a plane.
John took an aspirin.
John took a beating.
John took the job.
John took the match.
John took the food.
John took the picture.
John took my advice.

We could go on almost indefinitely. I hope that it is obvious that "take" means TRANSFER POSSESSION only some of the time. To find the correct meaning of a verb such as "take," it is necessary to examine the syntactic object of "take" and see what its properties are. If it is an object whose function is to TRANSFER LOCATION, then one strong possibility (though certainly not the only one—context is the ultimate determinant) is that "take"means "TRANSFER LOCATION by means of." Thus in "John took a plane," we are probably talking about TRANSFER LOCATION.

"Drinking," "eating," "breathing," and so on are all examples of INGESTION. We represent these by using what we know from our experiences about each event. Thus, the verb is specified by what is INGESTED and how. For example, "breathing" is INGESTION of air into the lungs; "eating" implies INGESTION of food through the mouth.

CONCLUDE is an action that represents the process of receiving an input either from memory or from outside, and producing an output which then becomes part of conscious thought. Verbs such as "figured out" imply a successful conclusion, "wonder" an unfinished one; and "decide," one based on choosing among alternatives.

THE UNDERSTANDING OF LANGUAGE

The understanding of language is a process whereby a person decodes a sentence, either read or heard, into a set of concepts that not only express the meaning of what was read, but are also the basic elements upon which the mind can operate. That is, after one decodes a message into concepts that can be used, an understander must attempt to use them. Thus, one must make inferences to find out what else is true, apart from what was just literally read.

Now that we have seen some of what language is like, we are ready to consider the nature of the reading process in more detail.

5 Early Reading Instruction: Predictions From Language

In trying to understand sentences, the key problem is the *analysis* of the incoming words, such that the end result is a meaning structure of the kind we have described. That is, in reading a sentence, our goal is to ascertain the meaning of that sentence and to connect its meaning to the rest of what we know and have just read. Theories of language that emphasize the role of syntax by studying the formal structure of language, tend to miss these crucial goals. Syntactic knowledge is of use in analyzing sentences. It is also of use in generating (or producing) sentences. But it is not the only thing that is of use. In analyzing sentences, we must not lose sight of the goal in focusing on the method. Our goal is to extract meanings from sentences. Syntactic information, semantic information, rules of reference, rules of inference, and world knowledge in general, all contribute to our achieving this goal.

In the history of instruction in language, the diagramming of sentences was once the rage. This practice required children to draw lines that divided up parts of a sentence and connected other parts of a sentence. We could make a similar mistake here. We could suggest that children learn to write the meaning structure for a sentence. This would, however, be a case of confusing "knowing how" with "knowing that."

We do not want to teach children to analyze sentences into meaning structures. They already know how to do that. They do it continually as they understand spoken English. We do, on the other hand, want them to learn to transfer to the reading situation the knowledge that they have about how to do meaning analysis. The lessons in this chapter exemplify how to do that.

PREDICTING OBJECTS

The six basic actions that we introduced in the last chapter all make strong semantic predictions as soon as they are identified by an understander. That is, as soon as we have understood that a TRANSFER OF INFORMATION is taking place, we know the following is also true:

The ACTOR is human.
The OBJECT is information.
The DIRECTION is human.

Now, as we have said, these predictions are not infallible. People do talk to walls. In some stories dogs talk. The key point is that the child already knows the kind of information listed above. That is, he knows the simple probabilities of what is likely to happen in the world around him.

Similarly, once we have determined that APPLY FORCE has taken place, we know that:

The ACTOR is capable of applying a force.
The OBJECT is something physical.
The DIRECTION specifies some place in the physical world or some object that has such a place.

In understanding a sentence, a reader, after identifying the underlying basic action, makes some assumptions. These assumptions include suppositions about the kind of relationships that will obtain between the remaining parts of the sentence and the place within the sentence that the concepts he is seeking are likely to be found. In other words, a reader makes both semantic and syntactic predictions as a result of his initial understanding of what he has read.

We can exploit this predictive ability in the teaching of reading by having children read sentences such as:

John threw the _____ to Mary.
Mary caught the _____.

The semantic predictions here are very strong. Of course, John could have thrown a bomb at Mary. But, the point is, by using his knowledge of language a child can learn to recognize words about which he already knows a great deal. Such semantic predictions are of great use in reading. For example, misspelled or illegible words written by hand still have to be read. We do this by predicting what the word is likely to be. Similarly, we can guess at the meaning of words we do not know by using our strong semantic predictions.

The way to exploit this knowledge is to ask children to fill in the blanks in sentences of the sort shown above. Here we are asking them to make a guess. In so doing they will learn that such guesses are valuable in determining the meaning of a word not yet part of their sight recognition vocabulary, but within their understanding vocabulary.

Below are further examples that exploit semantic predictions for objects. There are, of course, many acceptable responses for each of these examples. The objective is to show the child that he can know what a word might be before he has even seen it:

a. John pushed the heavy _____ to the wall.
b. Mary swung the _____ and then ran to the base.
c. Mary shoved the mean _____ in front of him.
d. John kicked the old _____ down the street.

TRANSFER OF POSSESSION

e. John gave Mary a shiny _____ for a present.
f. John bought a delicious _____ from the grocery store.

g. Mary took the _____ from the boy.

h. Mary got a _____ for what she did.

INGEST

i. John ate _____ at Burger King.

j. In the summer John likes to drink _____.

k. At the movies, Mary eats _____.

l. Mary breathed in the cool crisp _____.

After discussing the possibilities for what words can fill in the blanks, it is a good idea to have the children read a few sentences that contain different possible words for the blanks. Some of these should include words that are expected, and some should include words that might be less likely to occur in the above situations. Some should be within the sight-recognition vocabulary, and some should be new to the child. Here again, let me emphasize, "new" means new to the recognition vocabulary. The child should have all these words in his speaking vocabulary. From this exercise, the child learns to rely on his best guess. Have the children guess at words they don't know. They will be correct quite often, as long as they already know the word and have seen the surrounding context.

Some possible fillers are:

a. table	chair	sofa
b. bat	stick	club
c. boy	girl	troublemaker
d. can	toy	barrel
e. toy	apple	necklace
f. apple	banana	candy bar
g. ball	twig	hammer
h. prize	medal	spanking
i. hamburger	french fries	turnovers
j. soda	lemonade	punch
k. candy	popcorn	marshmallows
l. air	wind	smell

This lesson was designed with second graders in mind, but the principle can be exploited at any grade level. The words must all be known to the child. Learning to figure out what something says, when you have a good idea about its meaning, is not that hard. The words in the third column above are all readable by a child who can read their surrounding contexts, if his confidence in his predictive abilities is strong. They are, of course, less likely to occur than those in the first two columns and thus are less predictable. Ideally we want children to attempt the most predictable examples first.

DIRECTIONS AND RECIPIENTS

The same kinds of predictive abilities apply to directions and to recipients of the principal basic actions. Thus, TRANSFER OF LOCATION is always to a place; TRANSFER OF POSSESSION, to an animate object or institution; TRANSFER OF INFORMATION, to a person.

Here again a child can figure out a new word from the surrounding context, by means of the principles he has already learned:

TRANSFER OF LOCATION

> John went *home*.
> John walked to *school*.
> Mary skipped down the *street*.
> Mary rode around her *block*.

TRANSFER OF POSSESSION

> John gave the book back to the *library*.
> John took the chalk from the *teacher*.
> The teacher gave a star to the *student*.
> The policeman gave a ticket to the *driver*.

TRANSFER OF INFORMATION

> John yelled at his *brother*.
> Mother told *Father* about Billy.
> Mary saw the *batter* hit a home run.
> "It's time to go home," the teacher said to the *child*.

Here, the italicized words are, ideally, harder than the other words, although they should not always be harder. The child must learn to rely upon what he knows. He should achieve success should be easily, at least some of the time.

RESULTS AND REASONS

As we said earlier, a crucial part of the necessary structure of a sentence, or group of sentences, is what causes what. Here again, children already have a fair idea of what can cause what. What we want to do is encourage them to rely upon this knowledge. Having them choose between two words, neither of which they have seen, but only one of which makes causative sense, is one way to do this. What we are trying to do here is to teach children to sound out enough of the word they are attempting to read to allow their semantic predictions to fill in the rest for them:

John stood in front of the class. He was very _____.
  nervous   athletic
Mary hit the ball. It went over the _____.
  fence   pineapple
Sally bought a present for her Father. He was _____.
  punished   surprised
Jim did a bad thing. His mother said he would be _____.
  punished   watchful

The second choices here are intended to be both difficult to read and to make no sense in this context. If they were easy to read, a child could find the correct answer simply by the process of elimination. If they were sensible, then we run into the test-taking phenomenon of best guesses, which is irrelevant to learning how to read. But, when there is partial knowledge (in this case when the child can use what he knows about what is likely to be the meaning that makes sense here) he can use his ability to sound out words to help him recognize the meaningful answer. Thus, the child is not making a choice here. He should, because of his expectations, really only be able to read the correct answer.

What we want to do here is encourage a reliance on causative prediction. As the child improves in understanding what follows from what, his predictive sense can be honed directly. That is, in addition to teaching him to read new words, as the above examples are intended, we want the child to learn to rely on his predictions. We will see why this is necessary in the chapters that follow.

To enhance a child's predictive ability at this level, then, he should also have to choose between alternatives that are within his sight-recognition vocabulary, but only one of which logically follows from what he has read. We are not teaching him to read new words in the examples below. Unlike the previous exercise, in what follows he should already be able to read the words presented as choices. The idea is for him to guess about what makes causative sense. It is this ability that is the basis of how we understand complicated texts.

John hit a home run. He was very _____.
   happy   sad
Mary beat John in the race. He said she was the _____.
   fastest   sleepiest
Bill saw John's new book. He said he wanted to _____ it.
   read   burn
Fred was given a birthday present because it was his birthday. He was able to eat all the _____ he wanted.
   ice cream   peas

In each of these, either answer can be correct. The value of choosing the better answer is that the child learns to make predictions about what is implicit, since language does not usually make such inferences explicit. Part of the task of reading is to make such inferences. It is very important that children learn to rely on the "default" context. Texts rarely spell out all the details of what they describe.

6 Background Knowledge: Scripts

The key issue in comprehension, we have seen, is the application of appropriate knowledge to a situation. Such knowledge helps to fill in the details behind that situation. There are two primary issues related to such background knowledge:

1. Children cannot be expected to understand stories where they lack the background knowledge required to comprehend such stories.

2. Children can be taught to expand their background knowledge, and thus what they can read.

The point is that the *selection* of reading materials for children is crucial to their success in learning to read.

WHAT MATERIALS TO SELECT

What does a child know of the world? This is the key question to ask at any given point in teaching children to read. But it is a difficult question to answer for any one child. For a class, whose range of interests and backgrounds is likely to be wide, it borders on the impossible. Nonetheless, if we are to teach reading effectively in our schools, we must attempt to answer it.

One form of background knowledge that children have about the world is in the form of scripts. In this chapter I will introduce and explain the notion of scripts and then return to the problem of material selection.

SCRIPTS

The process of understanding stories relies heavily on our ability to extract what is implicitly true in a story or sequence of events. Think about what you are doing when you attempt to understand this simple story:

> John was hungry. He went into Goldstein's and ordered a pastrami sandwich. It was served to him quickly. He left the waitress a large tip.

Suppose that after reading this story, you were asked the following questions. How many of them would you have trouble answering?

> What is Goldstein's?
> What did John eat?
> Who made the sandwich?
> Who took John's order?
> Who served the sandwich?
> Why did John leave a large tip?

Most people have little trouble answering these questions. For the most part they are easy and have obvious answers. Any reading comprehension test that contained such a story would be considered simple. But the answers to these questions are not explicit in the story. At no point in the story does it say that Goldstein's is a restaurant (and probably a Jewish delicatessen), that John ate anything at all (let alone the pastrami sandwich that it seems so obvious he ate), or that the waitress brought the sandwich to John. Yet these answers are obvious. Why?

People understand more than they are told directly. They make inferences and add implicit information to the explicit information they receive. One important source of inferences is the knowledge of standard, everyday situations. People can read more into a story when they have experienced a situation similar to one described in the story.

What enables people to understand stories such as the one above is knowledge that is organized into structures that we call SCRIPTS (Schank and Abelson 1977; Cullingford, 1978). Scripts organize all the information we have in memory about how a commonplace occurrence (such as going to a restaurant) usually takes place. In addition, scripts point out what behavior is appropriate for a particular situation. Knowing that you are in a Restaurant Script leads to knowing that if you ask a waitress for food, she is likely to bring it. On the other hand, we know that if you ask her for a pair of shoes, or if you ask her for food while she is returning home on a bus, she is likely to react as if you had done something odd.

We use our knowledge of everyday situations to help us understand stories or discourse about those situations. We need not ask why somebody wants to see our ticket when we enter a theater, or why we should be quiet, or how long it is appropriate to sit in our seat. Knowledge of specific situations, such as theater-going, allows us to interpret the remarks that people make about theaters. Consider how difficult it would be to interpret "Second aisle on your right" without the detailed knowledge about theaters that the patron and usher share. It would be rather odd to respond "What about the second aisle on my right?" or "Where is my seat?" or "Is this how I get into the theater?" The usher simply takes the ticket and, assuming you understand and have specific knowledge about theaters, utters his otherwise cryptic remark without your saying anything.

Since people have learned to omit the details of an everyday scene, knowledge of the script involved enables us to replace the details in the story during understanding. For example, a story that refers to a script with ten events in it may explicitly state only the first and last of those events. That means we must infer the appropriate script. Being able to apply an appropriate script to a situation greatly simplifies the understanding process, because the script will tell us what *context* we are in. We call this process *script instantiation*.

We often leave out the obvious connections in a story. We do this as speakers because we assume that the hearer has a script available that will make things sensible. If such a script is not available, however, the hearer (or reader) will be confused. To see this, look at the following two stories:

> John went to a restaurant. He asked the waitress for the house special. He paid the check and left.

> John went to a park. He asked the midget for a mouse. He picked up the box and left.

In the second story we are unprepared for the reference to "the" midget rather than "a" midget and "the" box rather than "a" box. We also cannot figure out what the mouse and the box have to do with each other. The story does not reference a standard situation because we know of none that relate midgets, mouses, boxes, and parks. The story is thus not comprehensible, because we have no world knowledge that helps to connect its parts. If there were a standard "mouse-buying script" in which midgets in parks sold mice that were always packed in boxes, then we would be able to apply the script and connect the elements of the story.

What scripts do, then, it provide "connectivity." In the first story, which is superficially quite similar to the second, there is a great deal of connectivity. We are not surprised when "the" waitress or "the" check are mentioned. We understand exactly the relationship between asking for the house special and paying the check. We also assume that John ate the food that he was served, that he waited a while before being served, that he may have looked at a menu, and so on. All this information is brought up by the restaurant script.

Stories rely upon our knowing the smallest details of certain scripts, on occasion. For example, consider:

> John went into the restaurant. John ordered a Big Mac. He paid for it and found a nice park to eat in.

This story uses information that is part of the restaurant script that states that you don't have to eat inside a fast-food restaurant. However, if a reader does not understand that "Big Mac" refers to the fast-food part of the restaurant script, he will have difficulty understanding the story. The same story, with "coq au vin" substituted for "Big Mac," would seem rather odd. A story with this substitution would in principle be understandable, but the lack of applicability of available scripts would make it seem confusing.

So we see that although it is possible to understand a story without using a script, scripts are an important part of understanding many stories. They allow us to omit details when talking or writing, and fill them in when listening or reading.

Every script has a number of roles associated with it. When a story calls for a script, the actors in the story assume the roles that are designated by the script. When a particular script calls for a certain kind of actor, who has not been specifically mentioned in the story, his presence is assumed. This explains the use of the definite article in reference to "*the* waitress." She has been implicitly mentioned before, by virtue of the restaurant script being used.

The nature of the detail to be consciously inferred depends upon what script details (i.e., events in the script) are actually found in the story. Consider this story:

John went to a restaurant.
He ordered chicken.
He left a large tip.

A script is divided into *scenes*. The action of ordering brings to mind the ordering scene of the restaurant script. Because the entering scene is on the path to ordering, we assume that entering has already taken place when we hear about ordering. The events between ordering and tipping, as well as the final exit scenes, will be assumed as well. That is, we will have understood the story as if it had actually been:

John went to a restaurant.
He sat down.

He read a menu.
He ordered chicken.
He ate the chicken.
He left a large tip.
He paid the check.
He left the restaurant.

We fill in, as if we had actually heard them, the events of the script that were referenced. As long as we are simply filling in "ordering" to "tipping," it is safe to assume "sitting," "reading," and "eating." Since "tipping" is tied to "paying" and "leaving," we also assume these two actions.

But an understander does not want to assume too much when he is told of events that are far apart in the script. Thus the story "John went to a restaurant. He left." is a little odd. Do we want to assume that he ate? It is possible that John did eat in this story, but we simply might not want to assume it.

Deciding what is reasonable to assume about the events in a story is part of a reader's job. We must figure out from the script what steps have been left out. We must fill in the steps that surround the events that were specifically mentioned, by inferring the missing steps and treating them as if they had actually been stated.

Stories that are entirely script-based are not very interesting. An interesting story is not totally predictable. But a story in which the script goes awry in some way might be worth telling. Thus one important part of understanding is the understanding of stories that do not fit known scripts exactly but deviate from the norm in some way. A simple example of this is:

John went to a restaurant.
He sat down and signaled the waitress.
He got mad.
He left.

Such stories are what begin to make reading complicated. Here, a reader cannot assume that all of the standard events in the restaurant script have taken place. The entering scene and the beginning of the ordering scene occur quite normally. However, seeing "He got mad" stops us from processing the script in the normal fashion, because "getting mad" is not usually a part of the restaurant script. This deviation from the script alerts us to the fact that something outside the normal course of events is taking place (i.e., that the "interesting" part of the story is about to commence). Knowing the reasons for arousing anger, we know that often the cause is the action of some other person. The restaurant script tells us that usually at this point in the script, we expect the waitress to perform certain actions in a particular manner; we expect her to take an order and bring the food in a polite and relatively expeditious fashion. Because of John's anger, we assume that this in fact did not happen, causing John to become angry and leave the restaurant. Part of our understanding of this story is remembering the point in the script where the unexpected or non-script event took place. We do not want to infer that the rest of the events in the usual script occurred (i.e., that he paid the check before leaving).

The above inference is a weak one. John may have been angered by something unrelated to the script itself, but then the cause would probably have been mentioned explicitly. Here we must realize that stories are not usually intended to mislead readers. Normally we want people to understand what we mean. Thus, when something unusual occurs, we customarily mention it explicitly rather than leaving it for the reader to work out for himself. A good communicator does not make his listener work hard to understand his point, so the clearest course is usually the safest.

However, assessing what the story writer intended to be inferred is one of the hardest parts of reading. Unfortunately, it is that subtlety of expression, combined with deviation from the normal flow of a script, that makes a story worth reading. Determining what is going on in such stories is one of the hardest things to learn about reading. It is thus rather important to teach it.

Not all stories are script dominated. That is, understanding what script you are in is sometimes only useful for setting the background context. In understanding the above situations, scripts will only help us to a point. The point at which they cease to help is the point at which the unexpected (and thus the interesting) begins.

When only scripts, functioning normally, are present in a story, we have no real story at all. The following variants of the above stories, which involve script-based events only, are rather dull:

> John took the train to New York. He went to the smoking car to smoke a cigarette. He got off the train in New York.

> John flew to San Francisco. As they were coming in for a landing the stewardess said they had to put their seat backs up. John smiled and said, "Okay."

SCRIPT INTERACTIONS

One problem that occurs frequently in reading script-based stories is that sometimes there is more than one script involved. Multiple scripts in a story can cause many problems for a reader. Consider the following example:

> John was eating in a dining car.
> The train stopped short.
> John's soup spilled.

The first sentence activates two scripts simultaneously, RESTAU-RANT and TRAIN. When two scripts are active at one time, any new information can conceivably be a part of either of the two scripts. An adult reader would understand that the customer will probably ask for a replacement for the soup. We also understand that he might try to clean himself, and that the train personnel are likely to help. This information comes from various active scripts. But if you don't possess those scripts, it is unlikely that you will anticipate all this and be able to comprehend what ensues.

Another kind of script interaction arises at the point where one script leaves off and another begins. Consider this example:

John was robbed on the train.
At the restaurant he couldn't pay the check.

The robbery is an unpredicted event in the train script. It does not affect the normal completion of the train script, but it will affect any script that follows that involves money. In order to eat in a restaurant, it is necessary to have money. A reader must learn to recognize such potential problems, since story lines frequently depend upon them.

Another kind of script interaction takes place when script-endings are confused:

Yesterday John was in New York.
He went to a restaurant.
He ate a large lobster.
Then he bought a watch.

Here a reader must recognize when an active script has been ended and a new script has begun. Once the restaurant script has been started, we expect it to end in a normal fashion. Here it is ended implicitly by the beginning of another script that normally takes place in a different location. Recognizing such events is an important part of reading, and of understanding in general.

THE USE OF SCRIPTS IN TEACHING READING

Scripts relate to the teaching of reading both with respect to how we select reading materials and what we must teach when we teach reading. From the point of view of material selection, we must select stories that rely upon scripts the child knows. From the point of view of instruction, it is certainly advisable to teach him new ones, prior to reading any story that involves a new script. I will discuss the first issue here and the second one in Chapter 11.

MATERIAL SELECTION AND SCRIPTS

What scripts does a first or second grader know? First, let me point out that scripts are cultural indicators of the purest kind. Thus this question cannot be answered universally. It cannot even be answered for the United States. There exist many different subcultures in the United States. No one reading text will suffice for all regions of the country, since no region of the country, nor social strata within that region, shares the same scripts.

Farmers' children, for example, will know the "working chores of the farm" script. City children will know the "playing ball in the street" script. Suburban children will know the "going shopping at the mall" script, and so on. A story about school busses requires knowedge that children who walk to school may not have. A story on zoos is lost to children in rural areas. One on planes is lost to poor children, and one on farms is lost to city children.

I have taken the trouble of listing all the above story types because they all exist in children's literature. And every time one of them is presented, a whole segment of the child population may go to sleep or, worse, feel stupid and frustrated.

Imagine trying to understand the following story (taken from a fourth-grade reader) if you were very poor, very rich, had never been in a boat, never gone fishing, or even just had a limited knowledge of boats:

"I'm afraid you'll be swallowing some salt water before you get get a chance to catch any fish, Danny."

"What do you mean, Bert?"

"The boat is leaking and may sink any minute. Quick, use that can and start bailing out the water. I'll row back to shore."

"Hey, be careful not to splash with the oars. This is a new shirt. I don't want to get it wet!"

"Danny, how can you think of a shirt at a time like this, when the boat may sink?"

"I guess I just don't know what is important. Anyhow, there's no point in bailing. You are right; the boat is going to sink at any minute. It's almost completely underwater now."

"Let's get out and try to turn it over. We can hang on until help comes."

"Look, a motorboat is heading this way!"

"Too bad it didn't come sooner. I might have been able to keep my new shirt dry."

Selections of stories must be done with a particular culture in mind. Because it is a large segment of society, I shall concentrate on suburban middle-class American children. We can assume that such children live in one-family houses, have one or two cars in their garage, can ride a bike, and so on. Here are some scripts they are likely to have:

bicycle riding
going shopping in a car
eating in a fast-food restaurant
playing in the backyard
barbecuing in the backyard
family dinner at home
taking a car trip to visit relatives
going on vacation
staying at a motel

All of these, and a great many more, provide sufficient background for stories that a child can use in reading. Before showing how this is done, however, I would like to examine the scripts that a second child, this time a lower-class, poor, slum-dwelling child, is likely to have:

dealing with neighbors in an apartment house
hanging around on a street corner
opening a fire hydrant in the street in the summer
getting something at the corner store
finding out that something you cherish has been stolen

All of these will also provide backgrounds for stories, although they may not all be stories that suit middle-class tastes. But then not all children have middle-class tastes.

SUMMARY

The major point is that when we read, we frequently rely upon scripts that are derived from our experiences. Two things naturally follow from this. If we expect children to understand what they read, they must possess the script that the materials they are reading relies upon. Either we use the scripts that they already know, in the stories we ask them to read, or else we must teach them new scripts. We can, of course, do both.

7 Stories for Children: The Use of Scripts

If we are to design stories that will facilitate the teaching of reading, we must pay careful attention to what we intend to teach with such stories. Different things ought to be taught at different stages of development. In each stage, however, scripts known to the child should serve as the basic background.

Young children (3 to 6) are happy to listen to stories. But that does not necessarily indicate that they have a good idea of what a story is. After all, a story is an artifice that has never been explained to them as such. There is nothing inherent in the life of a child that requires stories. Stories are a means of entertainment for children. To expect that a child has a well developed sense of what makes up a story is similar to expecting a child to have a well developed notion of the structure of a television program. Children tend to have some ideas about the structure of both, but these do not necessarily correspond strongly to adult notions.

For example, consider some examples of stories made up by children:

(In the following, the child (H) is three and a half; P is the parent.)

P:Tell me a story.

H:I don't know what happened.

P:Once upon a time . . .

H:There was a little girl name Hana Rana Bana and she was riding her hot wheels (this didn't actually happen) and David Shapiro was riding a car and they went up and down the driveway into the backyard, zoom across, up the concrete.

P:Across what?

P:Papa taked a walk with David Shapiro and Hana Rana Bana and while she was riding and she stopped where the stop sign was with David Shapiro and Hana said, "David Shapiro, let's walk that way." They said, "Let's walk that way" (pointing opposite direction). They said, "Let's walk that way," so they went *that* way and soon they caught up and they turned the corner and turned and turned till they went, cause they were going on a real vacation, and they turned and turned and went on and on with Joshua and Hana Rana Bana and David Shapiro and soon they came to Gammy and Poppy's house and they gave lots of presents, even a ruler, even a drop of drippy drops and then they just were sleeping away at Gammy's and Poppy's house and had dinner and played everything, and then a new day they came to the Concord, they swimmed, and they played and they has lots of fun. So then after a while, they went home to their own house and they went to sleep, to play, that's all.

Here is another story told by the same child at age four:

P:Tell me a story.

H:Once upon a time there was a little girl and she lived with her mother and father in a big house, not an apartment house, and she was born in California. She has her own passport; her brother has a passport, too. Everyone has a passport, you know that, cause they have to have passports for special reasons. They went out to London and they had a good time there. They went riding on horses and they had real good times. They played. They brang lots of toys to play with, even books. Well, books are not such things to play with, you read them. And so then they went out, and then they saw a rabbit and they said hi to the rabbit, and then they said, would the rabbit be their pet. But the rabbit said it could not be their pet and then they came up to a kitten. They said to the kitten, "Could we have a kitten?" And then, after they had the kitten for their own, they named it, Joan, Joe, and then they walked on. The kitten was almost in danger. It got struck by a big wolf came and almost tried to bite it and then eat it, but it finally chased the wolf out and Mama and Papa got danger, Hana helped, Joshua was too little, he just said, "ah da" to the wolf. And then they came up to a great forest, they had lots of pine trees. And then they came up to something shiny with bright eyes, another kitten, instead it was a mother. And so, they took good care of the two kittens and then rode back to where they were and got, and then went to sleep, and after got dressed the next morning and went out to have their breakfast. They had Chinese breakfast, but Hana in case didn't bring the cat and left it outside by mistake, and Mama and Daddy locked it in cage. It was barking the next day, and meowing the next day, and then, away from danger, they saw balloons and then one bursted the balloon and then they got all the rest of the balloons. They had all the money that they needed for to buy a balloon. It was free. They didn't know that, so they paid some money. And then they got all the money that they paid. And then they went home to their own real house and wrote down that they had a good time and sended it to someone and everyone got a chance to read that. And then they had such good time, they had a jolly time here and from all you, this is telling the story. That's the end.

Clearly, while these stories share some superficial characteristics of stories, that is all they share.

Why then, have children read stories? The answer to this depends on the answer to why we teach children to read in the first place. I believe that there are a few primary reasons for acquiring an ability to read in our society.

1. The ability to follow printed directions is important in our society.
2. The ability to read textbooks for content is important for achieving a place in society.

3. The ability to read newspapers to keep oneself informed is important in our society.

4. Reading for entertainment is enjoyable.

Of course, there are a great many other reasons, but these four will do for our purposes.

Ideally then, we wish to teach children to read for each of the four reasons mentioned above. But we have a problem. With the exception of the first reason (following directions), all of them require that we first teach children to read stories. The explanation for this is as follows: We cannot reasonably expect young children to read newspapers when they have neither the background for them nor interest in them. Neither can we expect to excite them by reading dry texts, at whatever level of complexity. Thus we really have only one choice in the selection of reading materials. We should have children read stories that entertain them and motivate them to be proficient readers. Along with this, we can also have them read directions for answering questions, or otherwise responding to the stories they have read. But first we must teach them something about how to read stories.

STAGE 1: READING CONNECTED TEXT

The first lesson that a child must learn is that reading connected text is different from reading sentences in isolation. To teach this we use scripts that a child already knows and ask him to fill in implicit details about a story he has read. The following is a good example of what might profitably be taught at this stage:

Suburban Middle-Class Children

Johnny and his mother went to MacDonald's. They got fries and a shake. They had a good time.

1. What did Johnny eat?
2. What did Johnny drink?
3. Did Johnny sit down in MacDonald's?

4. How did Johnny get to MacDonald's?
5. How did Johnny feel later?

The aim of the lesson is for the child to infer what is going on. The answer to these questions are not one completely clear. The child must use what he has read and his knowledge of the MacDonald's script to give his best answer.

From this a child learns how to read between the lines. He also extends his recognition vocabulary (but again note that all the words are in his current speaking vocabulary). He also learns that his ideas can be right, yet others who have different answers can also be right. The answer to 4 is "drove," or "walked," or even "I don't know." They are all correct. The important point is to get the child to realize that he can legitimately infer what he believes to be true.

Lower-Class City Children

John and Bill were playing in the street. A man came by and said he would throw a ball with them. The kids had a good time. Later, they showed their mother some new tricks they had learned.
1. Where did John throw the ball?
2. Who did he throw a ball to?
3. Where was John's mother?
4. Why did the man throw the ball with them?

Here again, we have speculative questions. A child must learn to trust his inferences in reading. Thus, for example, question 3 may seem almost silly to an adult, but a child is happy to answer it when he is young; and he learns from this to rely upon his world model or script.

STAGE 2: ENABLEMENTS

The second stage in using scripts for the development of reading skills emphasizes the child's focusing on causal connections in a text. In particular, we want the child to trust his confusions as well as his successes.

Directions: Some of these stories do not make sense. Explain why:

John was playing in the yard. His father said he was going to cook steaks on the grill. "But the grill is broken," said John. "We don't have any steak," said his mother.

What is wrong here?

John rode his bike. The tire went flat. John's father used a stick to fix it.

Would this work?

Bill did not have any money. He wanted to go downtown. He got on the bus and went downtown.

What is wrong?

These stories cause a child to think about what is going on. Here again he must learn to trust his instincts about what is happening. Also, these stories will not work without the background script being present in the first place. No child can tell you about fixing a tire if he does not have a bike. He cannot deal with a bus story if he has never been on a bus.

STAGE 3: ASSESSING A GOAL

As I have said, a fundamental part of reading is assessing the goals of the characters. Since every script has in it an implicit goal, this is a good place to start.

John went to MacDonald's. He gave the man behind the counter a dollar.

1. Why did John go to MacDonald's?
2. Why did he give the man money?

3. Did the man want the money?

Bill was playing near the fire hydrant. "Let's open it up," said Fred. They had lots of fun.

1. Why did Fred want to open the hydrant?
2. What did they do when he opened it?
3. What time of year was it?

STAGE 4: BEGINNING A REAL STORY: SCRIPT FAILURES

Until now we have been using dull stories. This is a necessity in the early stages of reading, but it need not continue. It's important to move as quickly as possible to reading stories that look like stories. This serves two purposes. It captures a child's interest, and it begins to teach him, implicitly, what a story is like in its structure.

One method of doing this is to use script-based stories that do not go according to plan. It is quite common for a story to contain a snag or problem in a normal situation—thus forcing the main character (and the reader) to look for a resolution. This kind of story can best be taught in the context of well known scripts. The stories that I will use here to illustrate script failures are also dull, but this does not mean that such stories *must* be dull. I do not want to confuse the points that should be made here by adding story parts that are included for interest's sake only. Such trappings should be added for stories that children will read, as it is important to maintain their interest. The interests of the reader of this book, however, are presumably in the content surrounding the stories and not in the stories themselves.

John went to a restaurant with his mother. John ordered a hot dog. The waitress said they didn't have any.

1. What did the waitress say they didn't have?
2. What do you think John did when he heard that?
3. What would you do?

John was watching TV. All of a sudden there was a crash. Then the TV stopped working.

1. What do you think happened?
2. What should John do?

STAGE 5: SCRIPT INTERFERENCES

The next stage I will discuss is more complex than the previous four. In the actual use of scripts, real problems do come up that children know about. Resolving these problems is something they can use both to learn about stories and to help them learn to read. As always, what they know must guide what they read, not the other way around. (I will explain in Chapter 11 how and when children can start reading to learn rather than learning to read.)

John went shopping with his parents, but there were some problems. First, they had to get gas. Then they found that the toy John had picked out last week was all sold out. John was mad! Their shopping trip was cut short by a fire at a nearby store. John so enjoyed watching the firemen work that he forgot about the toy.

1. What happened to John when he went shopping?
2. Why was John annoyed at getting gas?
3. What made him even madder?
4. What made him feel better?
5. Do you think John had a good time?
6. Did he get what he wanted?

SUMMARY

To teach children to read, it is necessary to present them with stories that relate to what children already know. To do this, we rely upon scripts. Gradually we increase the complexity of the vocabulary and the unusual things that can happen within the background of the script.

When we teach reading we should ask the student to answer questions about what he has read. The questions should cause him to rely upon his own knowledge in addition to the actual content of the story he has read. As the stories increase in complexity, so do the kinds of inferences needed for understanding. The child is encouraged to guess, use his imagination, and really think about what's going on. No multiple choice answers can be used in such reading tasks, as they would entirely defeat the purpose of having the child rely on his own understanding. The child must be lead to look for explanations that use information that he already feels confident of. Picking one of several choices provided by someone else not only discourages such speculation but fails to teach the child how to make explicit what is implicit in a story. It is the explanation of the implicit that is the key to reading.

TEACHING SCRIPTS

The second issue raised at the beginning of the last chapter concerned the problem of how children accumulate a storehouse of scripts. Can we teach children scripts? Or, to put it another way, can we supplement the background knowledge that is so crucial for reading?

The answer to this is a qualified yes. To explain the qualifications, it is necessary to say something about the development of scripts in children.

ACQUIRING SCRIPTS

It is reasonable to wonder at this point how scripts are acquired. A simple example may suffice. Several years ago, I bought a new car. My daughter, Hana (then age 4), was with me when we bought it and asked me if I was going to buy a new key chain. I asked her what she meant. She replied that when we had gotten our old car in Rhode Island (where it had arrived off the boat 2 years earlier), I had bought a new key chain. This was her only experience with getting a car, but the events in it were a definite script for her. When you get a new car, you get a new key chain. If people are building scripts at such an early age, it seems easy to imagine that they possess an immense number of them.

(As an aside, it is worth considering the relationship between high-level knowledge structures such as scripts and the more common notion of an association. To argue that Hana's statement is just an association raises the question of association with what? Is it "new car," "buying car," "going to a place where there are many cars," or "changing the car we arrived in for a different one?" The answer is: all of the above. A script is a complex structure of knowledge and memories. "Associations" just do not explain this in any detail.)

Children begin to acquire scripts very early on. As the above incident shows, they often acquire quite erroneous or irrelevant ones. Nevertheless, ones that often recur become solidified in the child's mind. Underlying the construction of a script is the notion that things that have happened a certain way will happen that way again. Babies develop scripts that involve small details, (e.g. how they are held; or whether they are changed and then fed, or vice versa). An incident from an experience with my son illustrates this point.

My son Joshua, at age 4 months, showed a clear knowledge of certain scripts. One day when we returned from shopping, instead of opening the door, putting the stroller with Joshua in it inside, and then returning for the groceries, I reversed the order, putting the groceries in the house first. Joshua became extremely upset at this. Such "ritualization" is a well-known phenomenon with babies. Babies have many private scripts that become less important as they mature. It is hard to explain such scripts in terms of other factors. For example, Joshua was as comfortable in the front hall as on the front porch, being equally familiar with each, since on the way out of the house our script was usually reversed.

A child begins to develop what can be seen as a small version of an adult's script by experiencing again and again a bounded, named set of connected experiences. Even so, these "children's scripts" do not conform exactly to "adult scripts," as shown by the following:

Hana, age 3.4

P: Tell me a story—what happens in a restaurant? What happens—you go inside the restaurant . . .

H: You sit down, and you, uh, eat food.

P: How do you get the food?

H: From the waitress.

P: How does the waitress know what to give you?

H: If you ask for a hamburger, then she gives you a hamburger.

P: What happens if you ask for a hot dog? Do you get a hamburger?

H: No, you get a hot dog.

P: And then what happens after she gives you the food?

H: She gives you dessert.

P: And then what happens?

H: And then you leave.

P: And then you leave? Just like that?

H: No, the waitress gives you some money and you pass some money to her and she gives you some money back to you and then you leave.

Basically the child can put into a script what it understands of the situation that the script describes. My daughter didn't understand the money or business, and her script, although otherwise fairly accurate, reflects this lack of understanding.

The key point then is that children acquire useful scripts by experiencing a great many times a situation whose point they understand. To teach children new scripts requires not only giving the child a new experience, but repeating that experience often. The repetition tends to underscore the important elements of a situation, since they occur each time the situation is experienced (e.g., *eating* in the restaurant). The repetition also serves to eliminate the unimportant from the script. Thus a child who sees a waitress drop a tray in a restaurant will wait for that to recur each time and, when it doesn't, will eventually eliminate that event from its restaurant script (although still remembering it as an isolated event).

There are a number of ways to teach children scripts. One way is to create or act out new scripts in the classroom. The classroom is itself a script that the child is learning and modifying all the time. Reading materials concerning the classroom itself can serve as a source of many stories for which every child in the class will have sufficient (and equal) background.

A second way is field trips. This is now done to some extent, but it is important to do a great deal more of it, often repeating a particular trip a number of times. Remember that the more world knowledge the child has, the more the child can understand, and that world knowledge is derived from experience. Stories about the trip itself, or the particulars experienced on the trip, can then be read.

Lastly, scripts can be developed vicariously. However, these are the least useful scripts, because they lack the richness of detail provided by personal experience. We all have some idea of what things were like in Colonial times, for example, but the richness and depth of our knowledge does not compare with that of our personal experience. So, to teach a detailed part of some piece of world knowledge, it is best to personalize it as much as possible. Then a child will be more likely to make use of it in reading. One possibility is to have children act out plays about some piece of world knowledge they are to acquire. This will prepare them to read about a new subject by giving them their own experience to rely upon. In the end, it is the reliance on one's own experience that is the key to understanding. We understand in terms of what we have experienced.

This last point can be amplified. We like to think of ourselves as rational creatures who reason from sets of rules appropriate to the situations we encounter. But the evidence indicates otherwise. Experts who make decisions, surgeons in the operating room, judges imposing sentence, admissions officers of universities, all have rules they can cite as to what it is they should do in a given situation. But, an examination of their reasoning indicates that they are more likely to use a past experience to determine a present case. People don't buy a particular kind of car because their uncle had trouble with his, regardless of the statistics on the repair record of that model. We reason according to the particulars of our experience.

Children are no different. They use their own experience in what they do. This includes reading. If you expect a child truly to understand something, he, like an adult, must be able to draw upon his own experience in order to understand it. Reading and personal experience are strongly intertwined.

8

More Background Knowledge: Plans and Goals

All our knowledge is not contained in scripts. A great deal of what we know, and thus what helps us in reading, is in the form of knowledge about what someone is likely to do in a situation with which we are unfamiliar. Interesting stories, after all, do not deal with the mundane world that scripts represent. Interesting stories deal with novel situations, unusual problems, and clever ways of handling them. (These stories, of course, are frequently set against a mundane background that scripts can handle.)

Our ability to understand many stories depends on our ability to figure out a character's plans and goals (Schank and Abelson 1977; Wilensky, 1978). The assessment of the plans and goals of an actor in a story is an important part of what we must do when we read. In a sense, we must make guesses about the intentions behind actions in an unfolding story. These guesses help us to make sense of the story

Let's look at the following story:

John needed money for a down payment on a house.
He called his sister.

125

Scripts are standard sequences of events compiled from our experience. But it is unlikely that we have compiled something like a "paying for a house" script, and it is even more unlikely that we have a "borrowing from one's sister to buy a house" script. Nevertheless, we can understand quite a bit about what is implicit here. Understanding this paragraph would not be very different if "down payment" were changed to "son's education" or "paying off a bookie." In each case there is the general problem of raising money. In order to understand such stories, people make use of available knowledge about goals and the actions that can achieve those goals (in this case, that people often borrow money from relatives). This kind of knowledge is more general than scripts.

To use the knowledge one has about goals and plans, a reader must learn to recognize the implicit connections in a text. For example, a reader must know that stated goals are frequently followed by sentences that relate particular plans to the achievement of that goal. He must be able to interpret the second sentence above in the overall context of the original goal.

Let's look at another story:

John wanted to be captain of the baseball team.
He went to get a banana.

When we hear this story, we imagine that the second sentence will be a step in the main actor's plan to achieve the goal stated in the first sentence. We assume this without hearing a statement such as, "Now I am going to tell you about the plan that John used." We really have not understood the above story until we have tried to figure out how a banana can possibly help John obtain what he wants. In this story, we must conjure up an entire scenario in our minds before we can even begin to explain how the second sentence could be part of a plan to achieve the goal stated in the first sentence. (Sometimes this is too hard to do, and we become confused.) Two kinds of knowledge are needed to do this: knowledge of the fact that stories frequently require us to look for such explanations, and knowledge of the kinds of goals and plans that exist.

Fundamental to the reading process is our ability to assess the relation-ship between two sentences in terms of the kinds of plans and goals involved. For example, consider the following stories:

Mary wanted to cut her steak.
She called to John in the kitchen.

In this story, we have a goal, followed by a first step in a plan to achieve it. The problem for the reader is to recognize that relationship.

John was hungry.
He took out some ground beef.

Most readers find this an easy enough story to understand. But suppose story had been:

John was hungry.
He took out the Yellow Pages.

If only one rule applied to both stories, we might predict that John was about to cook and eat the Yellow Pages, in the second story. But no one really ever considers such a possibility when this story is presented by itself, as the Yellow Pages are usually seen as a source for finding restaurants.

To understand the second story, a reader must recognize that "hungry" means that a plan will (or should) be generated whose goal is to gain control of food. A reader must also know that one means of doing this is to go to a restaurant. This requires changing your location from where you are now to where the restaurant is. This in turn requires knowing where you are going, which may require a plan to determine what restaurant you want to go to and where it is. If we understand that the Yellow Pages contains a list of restaurants, it is possible to understand this story. Nevertheless, understanding it requires considerable effort.

Suppose we had heard instead:

John was hungry.
He took out Popular Mechanics.

We might wonder if there were some kind of restaurant guide in the back of the magazine or a relevant advertisement. We would have trouble understanding this story, because we have difficulty linking up the stated goal (satisfying hunger), with what seems to be a plan to achieve that goal (reading Popular Mechanics).

THE ELEMENTS OF PLANNING

If a reader is to assess the plans of characters in a story, he must rely on his specific knowledge of plans in general. If he lacks this knowledge, he will have difficulty understanding stories that implicitly use it.

John needed money.
He got a gun and went into a liquor store.

In such a story, a knowledgeable reader has no trouble understanding why John went into the liquor store. If the next line of the story were, "He got frightened and ran out," we would be able to answer questions about why he entered the store in the first place, and what may have frightened him once inside.

There are two main parts to understanding this kind of story. First, we must find the goals of the actors in the story. Second, we must ascertain the particular method (out of the set of methods that we know about) being used to realize each operating goal. This information is then used to tie the particular actions in the story to the goals (and the plans to achieve those goals) that the actions are intended to serve.

PLANNING

To see how people actually understand stories containing novel circumstances, we must ask ourselves how people deal with novel situations.

Suppose you want a book that someone else has. How can you get it?

You have a number of alternatives; which one you choose is dependent on your particular personality and circumstances (particularly financial circumstances in acquisition plans) and on your relationship with the possessor of the book. The first and simplest possibility is simply to ASK for the book. You might try this when the owner is your friend and the book is not too valuable. Another alternative is to EXPLAIN to the owner why you want or need the book. This might work if the reason is good enough. Still another possibility is to BARGAIN for the book. This can be done by offering money or another equally valuable object, or by offering to do a favor for the current owner, in payment.

Then there are nastier means. You could THREATEN the owner with physical harm if he doesn't give you the book. You could carry through with the threat, or simply not bother threatening and just OVERPOWER the current owner and take the book. Also, you could sneak around and STEAL the book while the owner was unaware of what was occurring.

The six plans written in upper case letters are the standard methods available for achieving the goal TAKE CONTROL. When we attempt to understand a story that involves someone trying to TAKE CONTROL of something, we can interpret his actions as an effort to satisfy the conditions necessary for using one of the above plans, or as being the implementation of one of those plans.

Four of the most common human goals are: ACQUIRE KNOW-LEDGE, CHANGE LOCATION, TAKE CONTROL, and GAIN SOCIAL CONTROL. Each of these goals requires the implementation of some set of plans. ACQUIRE KNOWLEDGE is the goal of knowing some fact. Once we know that someone needs to know something, we are aware of some of the standard plans for achieving that goal. Thus, we can understand ASKING, or a trip to the library. Often, realizing that someone needs to know something (e.g. understanding that opening a cookbook is preparation for cooking) is part of the problem.

To TAKE (physical) CONTROL of something we must persuade the current owner of the object to give it to us. Thus the plans, ASK, EXPLAIN, BARGAIN, and THREATEN are suitable for TAKE CONTROL. Since you might gain control of the object without either the knowledge or permission of the owner, or with his knowledge but without his permission, STEAL and OVERPOWER are also applicable.

The attainment of GAIN SOCIAL CONTROL (power or authority to do something) involves the same possible persuasive devices as the attainment of physical control. Some of the plans mentioned above are available, plus some new ones. There are two plans roughly analogous to STEAL and OVERPOWER that are useful here, namely, USURP and GO OVERHEAD.

Of all the plans, CHANGE LOCATION is the most "physical." That is, there are special mechanics involved in getting somewhere. Something other than mere persuasion is involved in changing the location of an object. Some available plans are: RIDE ANIMAL, USE VEHICLE, USE PUBLIC TRANSPORTATION, USE SELF.

The four plans we have just discussed do not exhaust the possibilities. Rather, they illustrate the most common kind of plans involving changing some state of the actor. Many other desired state changes do not require general planning mechanisms of this sort.

Consider, for example, the plan in the first story of this chapter, where John needs money for a down payment and decides to telephone his sister. The basic element of the plan is TAKE CONTROL (money). But what role does the phone call play? It relates to a condition that must be satisfied before any of the "persuade" plans can even begin. You can't persuade someone if you don't have a communication link with that person. When reading we must constantly postulate new goals, often of rather small import, that characters are likely to have and to pursue. Here, John might be said to desire the state change of establishing communications with his sister, which would help pave the way towards satisfying the more important goal.

IMPORT OF PLANS

An important skill in reading is the assessment of exactly why people are doing what they are doing. What purposes do they have in mind with respect to the actions that they are pursuing?

To teach children to read stories that involve planning, and most stories do, it is necessary to talk with children about how they would go about getting what they want. In reading any particular story, it is a good idea to discuss the available methods of obtaining what a character wants. Also, since we make character assessments from the choice of plan that the characters make in a story, ethical judgments about different kinds of plans must be discussed with children before they attempt to tackle such stories.

GOALS

In order to understand fully a person's plans, of course, it is necessary to understand the goal that a given plan is intended to achieve. As we have said, children's knowledge of adult goals is quite limited. For them to become effective readers, they must learn to understand why people want what they want, and why they do what they do to get it.

A reader must use his knowledge about what people are likely to want in order to interpret what they are doing and why they are doing it. To do this, an understander needs to know about all the goals people could have. However, if one were actually to set out to list all the different kinds of things that could be desired, there would be no end to it. One may be told, and be prepared to believe, that someone likes banging his head, or wants to line his patio with Martian rocks. One can accept these as idiosyncratic goals, whether or not they can be fit into some more general scheme. The real question for reading is: What goals can we assume a person to have when no explicit statement of goals is made?

Consider, for example, the following two stories:

John was walking in the park with his sweetheart, Mary. Suddenly, some boys jumped out from behind the bushes and held a knife to Mary's throat. They asked John for all his money. He gave it to them and they ran away.

John was walking in the park with his sweetheart, Mary. Suddenly, some boys jumped out from behind the bushes and held a knife to Mary's throat.

John laughed. The boys killed Mary and ran away. John picked up another girl in the park and went to the circus.

The first story is easy to understand. We do not even realize what assumptions about goals we are making when we read it. In the second story, however, our assumptions are quite clear, because they have been violated. When we are told that John loves Mary and knows she is in danger, we want to be able to assume that he has the goal of saving her. When we hear that someone has threatened Mary and demanded John's money, we must know that two goals are in conflict: preserving the health of Mary and preserving John's possessions. We expect John to have a value system that ranks the HEALTH of a loved one over his own POSSESSIONS (although we cannot be sure to what extent John believes that Mary's health is actually in danger). This knowledge is what allows us to interpret a sentence such as "He turned around and hit the robber" as a decision that indicates that preservation of possessions is very important to John (or that he thought the risk to Mary was slight). When we are asked "Why did John do that?" we can answer, "Probably he though he could protect himself this way and he didn't want to lose his wallet." This answer would come from a reliance on the standard goals we assume for most people. In the second story, we are upset as readers because all the expectations we have for how people should act (what goals they have) are violated. Our reactions to the second version of the story indicate the extent to which we use goals in processing—without being very aware of them (as was the case in the first story).

Let's look at some of the types of goals people have:

Satisfaction Goals. There exists a set of goals that we can safely assume all people (and animals) have. They come from biological needs and have a certain frequency with which they must be satisfied. Two obvious examples of satisfaction goals are hunger and sleep. There is a standard set of goal objects, or instruments used for achieving a goal (i.e., hamburger, bed, etc.).

If a person is trying to satisfy a satisfaction goal, such as hunger, through a particular goal object that becomes unattainable, we expect that some new goal object will be substituted for the first one. If John looks for a hamburger, but fails to find one, we predict that he will do something else to get fed, and will not merely forget about his hunger. This process of substituting different goal objects in order to satisfy a primary goal is called low-level goal substitution. Understanding that people readily make such low-level goal substitutions forces us to see Mary as a source of food in a story such as:

John was trying to find a hamburger place. When he couldn't, he called Mary.

Understanding this story means realizing that Mary will somehow help to feed John, rather than that John has changed his goal.

Satisfaction goals are extremely important in that they are basic to life. They also have a standard frequency of recurrence. We know that a person who has not eaten for an entire day is probably very hungry, and we would ordinarily expect him to do something about the situation. Thus when we hear that a satisfaction goal has been frustrated, we set up expectations about future actions, which helps us understand events that ensue. Therefore, we interpret this story:

John hadn't eaten for weeks. Finally he killed himself.

as being a more or less understandable reaction to a frustrated satisfaction goal. On the other hand, when we hear:

John hadn't jumped rope for weeks. Finally he decided to kill himself.

we find the story weird. Since jumping rope is not a satisfaction goal, we do not expect to see such a severe frustration reaction.

Enjoyment Goals. Sometimes people do things simply because they think they will enjoy doing them. We call such goals enjoyment goals. Examples might be travel, entertainment, exercise, or competition. The activities involved in satisfaction goals can also be pursued primarily for

enjoyment, as in "enjoy-eating." There are various goal-objects associated with enjoyment activities, but the primary way to plan for them is to
arrange to be physically present at the site where they occur. Low-level
goal substitution involves changing the site or even the type of activity
(e.g., going bowling if the movie is too crowded), provided the times scales
and expenses are comparable (i.e., you wouldn't decide to go to Europe if
the bowling alley were closed). For enjoyment goals, goal frustration
reactions typically are mild or moderate expressions of disappointment or
boredom. As a result, when enjoyment goals are frustrated, we cannot
easily predict future actions.

For example, consider the following:

John hadn't gone bowling for three weeks. He broke down and cried.

John didn't have enough money to go to the movies. He called up Mary and
went for a walk instead.

The goal frustration reaction for enjoyment goals is normally mild.
Knowing this is what causes us to find the "bowling" reaction funny.
When enjoyment goals are frustrated, we expect people to find alternative
pleasures, or to be a bit unhappy. Any other reaction seems abnormal.
Such knowledge allows a reader to conclude from a story such as:

John shot Mary when she wouldn't go to the movies with him.

that there is something wrong with John. Such decisions are, of course,
very subjective, but they are nonetheless an important part of how we
understand the world around us, and they thus constitute a major aspect of
the reading process.

Achievement Goals. People also have the goal of achieving certain
positions or of owning certain properties. Some common achievement
goals are: possession, power position, good job, social relationship, skill.
When achievement goals are satisfied, they typically guarantee the future
satisfaction of a variety of satisfaction goals and enjoyment goals. If you
are rich or powerful, higher goals are much easier to satisfy. Low-level

goal substitution does not occur very readily with some achievement goals. Someone who wants to own a dozen original Rembrandts may not be satisfied with a dozen Renoirs. John, who wants to marry Mary, is probably unprepared to marry Alice instead.

Frustration reactions to achievement goals often lead to a withdrawal on the part of the frustrated actor. This is often accompanied by the establishment of a new, unrelated high-level goal that is some way compensates for the frustration. An example of such a high-level switches in goals might be trying to be more professionally successful than a rival who has won your love object. Much of what we understand depends on predictions we can make about the kinds of things people usually need to achieve. For example, we can predict that people need at least one job, the loss of which will cause them to seek another.

People choose substitute goals for various reasons. For example, availability, difficulty, importance, and pleasure to be obtained, all enter into a decision to seek a given object or position. Any potential goal object is assessed according to these factors.

Decisions about possible substitutions depend on the similarity of the substitute, based on the factors that are important to the actor. Thus, the story:

> John wanted to buy a fancy stereo, but none were good enough. He settled on a new TV instead.

makes sense, but this one does not:

> John wanted to buy a fancy stereo, but none were good enough. He got a new pair of shoes instead.

The important issue here is the similarity of these objects, on the basis of the factors mentioned above. Stereos and TVs are goal objects that satisfy entertainment goals. They thus have much in common. Stereos and shoes are, for most people, unrelated, from the perspective of the goals they share. Understanding the latter story requires us to make an unusual assessment about John. We must conclude that simply getting something new pleases him, or else we can conclude that in his value system, and perhaps in his culture, these two items are somehow related in value. Perhaps they both can be shown off to great approval. Of course, values are rather subjective; not everyone feels the same way about every object. Understanding a person means, to some extent, being able to understand his actions. That is, when we know a person's goals and values, we can make better judgments about the meaning and intent of what he does. In reading we are constantly called upon to do this, if we are to understand what follows, because understanding character development is crucial to the understanding of short stories or novels.

Preservation Goals. People actually spend a good deal more of their time preserving or maintaining what they have than in attempting to achieve new goals. Another important kind of goal, therefore, is a preservation goal. Preservation goals are set up by people to maintain the health, safety, or good condition of people, positions, or properties, once such positions or states are attained.

When you have something of value, you act so as to keep it. Sometimes, though, a preservation goal may pertain to something you've had all your life, such as good eyesight. The pursuit of preservation goals leads to plans of a different character than those for other kinds of goals. To maintain something, you must understand the nature of possible threats to it, and act so as to anticipate them. Threats come in three forms: the plans of others, discrete acts of Nature, and the erosion of time. The most interesting of these are the plans of others.

Consider the plan of someone whom you expect to try to take some possession X of yours from you. His plan for obtaining this object involves knowing where it is, going there, and taking control of it. To block this you must prevent or interfere with at least one of these goals, or the necessary preconditions of their subplans (if you know what they are). You must formulate an ANTI-PLAN (Carbonell, 1979). Perhaps you will hide X, to prevent his knowing where it is; or perhaps you will guard access to it, so that he can't get to it. Anti-plans require continued vigilance, as the opponent may adopt an anti-anti-plan, and so on. Thus the success of preservation goals tends not to be clear and final (barring the opponent's goal change, or his disablement).

Preservation goals involving protecting something from the slow ravages of time have the property that low-level substitution is often determined more by resource limitations such as time and money than by the content of what is being maintained. Usually, the desire or need to protect and maintain something valuable, such as a house, is a constant, every-present goal. ("John wanted to mow his lawn, but when he couldn't, he cleaned out the garage.")

Failure of a preservation goal may lead to being upset, which people often deal with by establishing a new achievement goal to restore or regain the damaged or lost object, or replace it. Predicting such a response depends on the value and type of object that was lost. Thus if you lose your house, you can be expected to buy a new one. If you lose a memento of a trip, it is unlikely that you will make the same trip again to replace the momento.

The frustration-reaction for a preservation goal is in many cases taken care of by a script, such as the automobile-insurance script, the roof repair script, etc. Low-level goal substitution does not occur for achievement goals that are initiated as a result of the frustration of preservation goals. For example, it does not make sense to say "John wanted to find his lost diamond stick pin, but when he couldn't, he found his gloves instead."

Crisis goals. Crisis goals are a special class of preservation goals that are set up to handle serious and imminent threats to valued persons and objects, such as serious illness, fires, or storms. Crisis goals often arise suddenly, often unexpectedly, and have a high priority. In contrast to preservation goals, which deal with potential threats, the threatening agent (human or natural) in a crisis situation is active at the moment. The methods used for achieving crisis goals tend to be scripts, such as the call-the-ambulance script, or the evacuate-the-building script. There is usually not enough time or calm during emergencies for much planning. Low-level goal substitution does not ordinarily occur with crisis goals, because the threat is usually highly specific. It would be absurd to say, "John couldn't get Mary to the hospital in time, so he put out a fire." Emotional reaction to the failure of a crisis goal is often shock, while the reaction to the success of a crisis goal is usually intense relief.

Instrumental Goals. Any goal that, when achieved, helps the pursuit of another goal, but does not in and of itself produce satisfaction, is called an instrumental goal. All of the other goals discussed so far can make use of an instrumental goal; sometimes instrumental goals are used to serve some combination of other goals. For example, if John and Mary want to go to the movies (an enjoyment goal), but also wish to protect their small children (a preservation goal), they will probably have an intermediate (or instrumental) goal of finding a baby sitter.

An instrumental goal can be characterized by the statement "I have to do X in order to do Y." Because many different kinds of scripts can be used to achieve an instrumental goal, it is difficult to make generalizations about them. It is also very common for people to make many low-level substitutions regarding instrumental goals, since the instrumental goal is merely a step in a plan to attain some other, more important, goal. For example, if John and Mary couldn't find a babysitter, they might take the kids to their parents' house, or go to a drive-in movie with the kids. The instrumental goal of finding a baby sitter was merely a means to some other end.

When an instrumental goal is frustrated, the reaction tends to be agitation or anger, because if the instrumental goal is not achieved, the other, more important goal also cannot be achieved. If the other goal is important enough (say a crisis goal), continual frustration of all possible instrumental goals could lead to an extremely intense reaction to what ordinarily would seem a minor set-back. ("When the Third National Bank denied John the loan, he shot himself.")

GOAL PRECEDENCES

When many goals are potentially active at one time, people need rules for deciding what takes precedence. Children must be taught in reading to look for the strategy that a character is pursuing. They must learn to evaluate whether a plan of action is a good one, and what its likely results might be. As I have said, the ability to predict what will happen next is a very important part of reading. Such predictions come in part from our expectations about normal actions and goals in a given situation. Below are some of the rules people normally use:

1. Crisis goals tend to take precedence over satisfaction goals. It would be strange for a person to eat while somebody was robbing him, no matter how hungry he was. We expect actors to preserve what they have when it is threatened before they go about attempting to satisfy a common, recurring satisfaction goal. The satisfaction goal will wait or will appear again, and thus has less urgency than a crisis goal. A sentence such as "Walter refused to eat the eggs in front of him because he was allergic to them," is understandable as a crisis goal, where concern about health takes precedence over a satisfaction goal of desiring to eat. A person drinking sea water when he is very thirsty is obviously in violation of this principle. We know this because we expect an adverse effect on the health of the person drinking sea water, and we assume that the person must have been in a confused or desperate state of mind to have taken such a chance. We do not expect preservation goals to take precedence over satisfaction goals. Thus is someone said, "I can't have dinner tonight; I have to get a lock for the basement window," we would have to conclude that there was a threat of an imminent break-in. That is, we would have to conclude that installing a lock was a crisis goal rather than a preservation goal.

2. Satisfaction goals usually take precedence over achievement goals. Of course, it is common to hear statements such as "John was too busy to eat," but sentences such as this indicate a temporary situation only. During a crisis, satisfaction goals will be suppressed while the crisis goal is taken care of immediately. When satisfaction goals are suppressed in favor of achievement goals, this also is only temporary. Eventually John will stop working and eat, or sleep, or whatever, because the satisfaction goal will have become too demanding.

3. People tend to take care of enjoyment goals (and preservation goals, to some extent) when crisis goals are not present, and when satisfaction

and achievement goals are not of great importance at the moment. If, however, we learn that someone is continually at the race track, watching old movies, or waxing his automobile at the expense of his job and his family, then we must conclude that an enjoyable activity has become an addiction, and has taken on the cyclical character of a satisfaction goal.

4. Instrumental goals, because they are so closely connected to other goals, take on the precedence rules of the goals they serve. Thus an instrumental goal connected to a crisis goal will have very high priority, but an instrumental goal connected to an enjoyment goal will have generally low priority. It is odd to hear, "While dashing to find water to put out an office fire, John stopped to buy a candy bar," but it is reasonable to hear, "While going downtown to buy tickets for a show, John stopped to buy a candy bar."

5. All goals have a period of activity. Satisfaction goals are cyclical, and recur at set intervals, becoming more demanding the longer they wait to be fulfilled. Crisis goals need to be handled immediately. Achievement goals have fixed periods of activation for each individual goal. If they are not activated, they tend to decrease in urgency and sometimes disappear altogether. For example, a person who hsa been unable to gain admission into medical school over a period of a few years might substitute biological research as a career. Preservation goals and enjoyment goals were discussed in point 3 above. People's reactions to a goal frustration tend to be highly active for a short period, even to the point of taking precedence over all other goals. A robbery victim is probably more interested in calling the police than in eating. Time heals, however, and the urgency of a reaction to a blocked goal will fade and be replaced by other goals as the frustration decreases.

GOALS AND BELIEFS

Where do goals come from? Sometimes goals come in standard packages associated with some property of a person. For example, a lawyer can be expected to have a set of goals in common with other lawyers.

However, not all goals occur in standardized packages. Many goals, or reactions to goals, occur in response to some input outside of any standardized situation. These goals or reactions can be predicted solely on the basis of the human qualities of the actors involved in the situation. Most humans can be assumed to share, to some degree, a basic set of beliefs about how to behave, or about why others behave in certain ways, in given situations. That is, in order to determine what goals an individual is likely to have at any given time, it is necessary to have available a set of beliefs about what an individual is likely to want in a given circumstance.

Consider the following story, which is the synopsis of a soap opera:

> John and Mary miss Billy very much now that he and Mrs. Parker are on the West Coast. Mary is having a hard time reconciling herself to the loss. Phyllis has suggested Mary take a job on her father's newspaper, but Mary says no. Carole and Ken are having a bad time of it and Carole is wondering if she should give up her classes in order to save her marriage.

> Frances is so intent on having Don as a son-in-law, she is giving her daughter, Helen, an all expense-paid trip to Monticello. Helen doubts the effort is worth the possible gain, but Frances is determined that Helen ensnare Don.

Let's look at the implicit goals and belief rules that are assumed here:

1. When separated from them, people miss those they like.
2. People have trouble adjusting to new situations.
3. People want to maintain good emotional relationships.
4. Marriages are worth maintaining, but only if the cost isn't too high.
5. High costs (hassles) are to be avoided.
6. Saving a marriage requires time.
7. To find time to do something, stop doing something else.
8. People give up less valued things for more valued ones.
9. To induce someone to do something, a person can influence them with gifts.

10. It is unreasonable to work harder for something than that thing is worth.
11. People want their children to have advantageous marriages.

There are actually more rules present here than just these eleven, but these are good examples of the kinds of beliefs that people operate with daily and assume that others operate with. Having such rules available is an important part of our ability to understand, and hence they are crucial in reading. Children must learn to extract the beliefs inherent in what they read. They must learn to use their own beliefs to interpret what they read. And, they must be able to figure out, from confusing stories like the one given above, what a character is likely to want, and what is is likely to do to get what he wants.

SUMMARY

We can see, then, that an extremely important part of reading is the ability to assess what a character wants; what plans he might make to get what he wants; how an action he performs relates to any plan that he has developed; and what he might do if things go awry. We also want to know, as readers, why a character has made a particular choice, what that tells us about the kind of person he is, and what he might be expected to do in the future.

Reading depends strongly upon our ability to make these assessments. We learn to do this almost randomly in our society. The ability to track plans and goals is a crucial aspect of reading, yet is is really not taught in school at all. Clearly, it ought to be.

9 Stories for Children: Using Plans and Goals

The concept of planning to achieve a goal can be much more easily and directly taught to children than the parallel exercise of attempting to provide children with additional scripts. Scripts are really only acquired by experience, as we have said. But plans, once understood, can be abstracted from one situation and used in another. Thus their use is less dependent on experience. Plans are usually quite general.

To teach children to track plans while reading, we must address ourselves to three issues:

1. Teaching children to read stories that involve plans and goals.
2. Teaching children how to plan to achieve a goal.
3. Teaching children about goal conflicts, resolutions, and other aspects of stories.

As we did with scripts, we can create a progression of stages in the complexity of stories that we use that rely upon plans and goals.

STAGE 1: CONNECTED TEXT

The first thing to teach with respect to stories involving plans and goals is that stories do in fact involve such things. This presents a different problem than the one we had with scripts. Children need not be taught that stories involve scripts. They know all they need to know about scripts (in the sense of "knowing how" discussed earlier). The issue there was to encourage them to rely on their existing knowledge to make predictions and fill in implicit information.

The situation with plans and goals is somewhat different. As with scripts, children already "know how"; they *can* plan, *do* have goals, and thus know something of what there is to know about plans and goals. But their goals are very simple, their plans even more so. Thus our task with plans and goals is both to teach children how to use them in reading, and to teach them explicitly what they are and how they function.

The first step is to accustom children to reading stories in which the relationship between sentences in the text is one of plan to goal:

A. Johnny was very hungry. He opened a cook book.
B. Johnny was very hungry. He opened the cupboard.
C. Johnny was very hungry. He got on his bicycle.
D. Johnny was very hungry. He lit the oven.
E. Johnny was very hungry. He called to his mother.
F. Johnny was very hungry. He got some money from his piggy bank.

These six stories, and others like them that can be easily developed, illustrate the first step in plan-goal connection in reading. It is the job of the teacher here to discuss with the children the options available in a situation, and how the second sentence in each story relates to the goal set up in the first sentence. But, the teacher need not teach children about goal classifications. The list that follows is for teachers to use in focussing on the objectives in teaching. The relationships inherent in these sentences are as follows:

A. *Gain Knowledge.* To achieve a goal, it is sometimes necessary to have more knowledge about how to achieve it. This is the relationship of cookbook to hunger.

B. *Enablements.* Often gaining control of an object requires doing something that might otherwise be seen as irrelevant. Here opening the cupboard is relevant, if we assume that the cupboard contains food. This opening enables the "gain control" plan to operate.

C. *Gain Proximity.* To satisfy a goal, it is often necessary to move to where the satisfacton can take place. Here we must assume that Johnny is going to some kind of eating place.

D. *Preparation.* Even when all elements are present (i.e., we know what to do, have control of the goal objects, and are in the right place), certain preparatory steps must be taken. Here lighting the oven is part of that preparatory procedure.

E. *Getting an Agent.* We need not do everything for ourselves. Sometimes others, especially mothers, will do it for us. Of course, they are only assistants in a plan; ultimately, we will have to eat for ourselves.

F. *Planning Ahead.* Often a plan involves multiple steps. Going to a restaurant without taking money or knowing how to get there can be a problem. Here Johnny is planning ahead for a goal that we can guess (eating ice cream?).

The key issue in Stage 1 is explaining to the student how sentences can convey steps in a plan. To do this, a child must have a good idea of how to plan to achieve a goal. Quite often children don't plan, however. Usually they have a script available to help them through a situation. This is most likely to be true in common situations, such as hunger. The best way to explain sentences that indicate steps in a plan is to use stories that involve novel situations. The questions that should be asked of children about the above stories include:

1. Why did Johnny do what he did?
2. What else could he have done?

3. How well did his actions help him get what he wants?
4. What will he do next?

Keep in mind, here again, that the theoretical elements need not be taught explicitly. It makes no sense to teach a theory of the construction of plans than it does to teach a theory of grammar. Children should not be asked to underline enablements or categorize actions in terms of planning. Knowing how to use such information, not knowing the information explicitly, is what is important here. If the child can answer the above questions, he has understood.

STAGE 2. ENABLEMENTS

As with script-based stories, the next stage in reading stories based on plans and goals is helping the child to recognize that actions can enable a plan or goal to take place. It is crucial to reading to recognize that an action was performed to facilitate the accomplishing of a desired plan or goal. Here are some examples:

Johnny wanted a new baseball glove. When Johnny's father got home, Johnny greeted him at the door with a big hug. Then he asked his father if he wanted to play catch.

Why did Johnny greet his father in the way he did?
Why do you think Johnny wanted to play catch?
What do you think will happen when they play catch?
What would you do if you wanted a new baseball glove?

Susie was jumping rope with Jane. She was tired and she wanted to quit. But Jane hadn't had her turn yet. Suddenly, Susie yelled that her ankle hurt.

Why couldn't Susie quit?
Did Susie's ankle really hurt?
Why did she say it did?

How do you think Jane will feel?
What kind of person is Susie?

Each of these stories involves situations in which a child has a goal. In both cases the goals are stated and obvious. Children must learn to see how someone can plan a course of action to achieve a goal. In both of these stories the children do not take the most direct course of action. Children must be taught to recognize the course of action, or plan, that is being followed. In addition, they must attempt to understand why the direct course of action is not being followed. This aspect of understanding, namely, character assessment, is crucial in reading, since it is a source of future predictions.

For example, once we find that a character has acted dishonestly, we can expect him to do so again. The following is taken from the Treasure Island story used in Chapter 3:

> Silver went over to talk with the pirates. They laughed together. Then he saw Jim. Jim asked who the men were that Silver had laughed with. Silver said, "What men?"

Such stories provide good opportunities to discuss issues such as guilt by association, the combination of bad traits, and so on. In stories, we are rarely told something that isn't intended to set up something else. Children must be taught to look for these clues in texts, to guide them in their predictions about actions and their consequences.

STAGE 3: ASSESSING A GOAL

In discussing scripts, we noted that the third stage in the progression of script-dependent reading material was to assess the goal underlying the script. The same can be done when a series of actions has no overtly stated goal. As readers, we learn to figure out what goal is being pursued.

> Jane left the house quietly. She had all her money with her. At last she was at the store. She went in. It was a store that sold pipes. But they were all so expensive.

What is Jane planning on doing?
Why do you think she is doing that?
What is the difficulty in achieving her goal?
What can she do about it?

In such stories, it is often a good idea to have the child answer questions like those above, and then to proceed with the rest of the story. For example, the story could continue:

How was she going to get her father his birthday present? Then she thought that her older sister might help. She hurried home.

This can be followed by more questions about likely future actions. Children must learn to figure out why people do what they do. They must also learn to recognize that a story can mislead them; they can make a wrong guess, and still recover.

Bill called up John and asked him to go with him to the movies. John was sad. Everyone had forgotten his birthday. He agreed to go.

Here the usual goal-related questions can be asked. Then we continue:

But, just as they arrived at the theater, Bill remembered he had locked his dog in the house. He said he had to go home.

Here there is a break in the story. Have the children discuss it. Have them speculate on what Bill might be doing. Have them talk about how John may feel.

A reader comes to expect that conflicts in stories will be resolved. Have the children talk about what their expectations were and what they are now. Then the story can be completed:

John agreed to go back to Bill's house, but he was miserable. When they entered Bill's house, there was a big shout of "surprise." All of John's friends were there.

STAGE 4: PLAN FAILURE AND GOAL BLOCKAGE

Many stories revolve around difficulties in planning or difficulties in achieving a goal. Reading such stories often involves recognizing that a plan has failed or that a goal has been blocked. Then we can recognize future actions as part of new plans or goals:

> Susie got on her bicycle. It was a beautiful day. She started to ride, but the bike was going very strangely. She couldn't ride after all. Her sister yelled to her that her tire was flat. She felt awful. But her sister was a nice sister. She offered Susie her own bike.

> What did Susie want to do?
> What prevented it?
> Did Susie get to do what she wanted?

> Joe Bear was hungry. He asked Irving Bird if he knew where some honey was. Irving said he'd tell if Joe brought him a worm. Joe said he'd be happy to but he didn't know where any worms were.

> What was Joe's plan?
> Could Irving help?
> Why did Irving do what he did?
> What do you think Joe will do now?

Actually, the above story is rather complicated. It involves one character willfully blocking another's goals for ulterior motives. Such motives lurk behind many a tale, and it is important for children to learn to recognize them.

STAGE 5: COUNTERPLANNING AND GOAL COMPETITION

In real life, there are a great many times when we want what someone else also wants. Children encounter this too. A great many stories are based on goal competition and the means of achieving a compromise or achieving outright success. These kinds of stories are easy to find and sometimes very realistic.

One example of this kind of story is from Aesop:

> Once upon a time, there was a dishonest Fox who lived in a cave, and a vain and trusting Crow who lived in an elm tree. The Crow had gotten a piece of cheese and was holding it in his mouth. One day, the Fox walked from his cave, across the meadow, to the elm tree. He saw the Crow and the cheese and became hungry. He decided that he might get the cheese if the Crow spoke, so he told the Crow that he like his singing very much and wanted to hear him sing. The Crow was very pleased with the Fox and began to sing. The cheese fell out of his mouth, down to the ground. The Fox picked up the cheese and told the Crow that he was stupid. The Crow was angry and didn't trust the Fox anymore. The Fox returned to his cave.

> What did the Fox want?
> What did the Crow want?
> Why did the Fox ask the Crow to sing?
> Why did the Crow sing?
> Who won?
> What would you have done if you were the Fox?
> What would you have done if you were the Crow?

Here we have a series of plans and counterplans, all in pursuit of the same goal object. Children can easily understand such stories because they can relate to them. Therefore, such stories should be used as a basis for teaching more complex or subtle stories.

> Mugs knew that the gold was hidden in the safe. Bugs was guarding the safe. He knew Mugs wanted the gold. But Mugs knew that Bugs loved chocolate. He offed him some. But Bugs was too smart. He said, "I can see you are just trying to get me away from the safe." Mugs said that wasn't true at all. They talked for a long while about it. Later Mugs went home and counted the gold that his partner Jugs had gotten.

> What happened?

What was Mugs' plan?
What was Bugs' plan?
What was Jugs' plan?
What did Bugs think Mugs' plan was?

This story is rather complicated for a child so it may be a good idea to explain it to the child. The child may need to be taught explicitly about planning and counterplanning. Explain what Mugs may have been doing here and then have the children read more stories until they get the idea.

SUMMARY

The purpose in systematically teaching children about goals and plans is to lead them to make the appropriate assumptions, create the right expectations, draw sensible conclusions, and otherwise try to tie together what they have read. Many of the questions I have proposed here are currently being asked of children in reading comprehension instruction. But, for the most part, they are being asked randomly and unsystematically. Thus, although a child might occasionally have to speculate on some aspect of what he has read, because of these questions, he is not systematically learning to ask these kinds of questions of himself as he reads. And that is what he must do if he is to learn to understand.

10 What Not To Teach

Let us now consider the tools and methods presently employed in the teaching of reading in light of what we have said so far. How relevant are present teaching methods to the needs of a developing reader?

Many children spend the time in school that is supposed to be devoted to teaching reading by going through a workbook at their own pace. Such reading workbooks consist of about one hundren pages of tests. These tests, depending on grade level, involve stories to be read with questions to be answered about sentences or words, word meanings, syllabification, prefixes, and a great many other things. Calling this process of answering tests in a workbook "learning to read" is a misnomer. What a child is probably learning during his reading period is how to take tests.

In a test-oriented society, learning to take tests is very important. Children using such workbooks will undoubtedly do better on their College Boards than those who do not use such books. But, if training is to be given for such tests, it would probably be more profitable to give explicit instruction in test-taking rather than to include it in a reading lesson.

Do these tests help to teach reading? It seems unlikely. Some sample questions, typical of the type of questions found in many fourth grade readers, illustrate why this is so.

Circle the word synonymous with the underlined word.
1. Mrs. Smith went to the *pharmacist* to buy aspirin and vitamins.

      doctor   druggist   gift shop

2. Joan wanted to be a *secretary* for a doctor in a small office.

      helper   secret   plumber

3. The glass was so *fragile* that Mary's mother wouldn't let her hold it.

      old   breakable   faded

What is the child supposed to be learning from such questions? Is it possible to learn new vocabulary from them, for example? At first glance, it seems reasonable to supose that such examples might be an effective method of teaching vocabulary. After all, we can learn new words from reading them in context. But, isolated sentences do not really provide enough context. Further, the task one is engaged in is an important part of the context that helps us to attempt to figure out what we need to find out about a word. We need to know everything about a word to understand its use in a given sentence. It is very difficult to learn new words from reading them in sentences when the sole purpose in reading those sentences is to circle a "correct" answer. In that case, the child needs to know, not the meaning of the word, but enough about the meaning of the surrounding words to discern the correct answer.

A futher problem is that the child has not had to learn the sound of the word at all. Clearly what the child is being asked to do here is make a best guess about the right answer. He need not even look at "pharmacist" to know that the right answer is "druggist." In fact, the association of pharmacist-druggist need never be made at all by the child.

Let's consider example 2, where the vocabulary item in question, "secretary" is likely to be known by the average fourth grader. One thing that is being shown (probably inadvertently) is that the suffix "-ary" has no meaning in English in general. This is illustrated in the test itself by the use of "secret" as one of the possible answers. (This example appeared in a section of the reading text labeled 'words ending in "ary."') The child's task, after discarding the premise that Joan wished to grow up to be a secret, is to determine whether a secretary is a helper or a cook. The choice is obvious is you know the meaning of the word and impossible if you do not. Furthermore, the correct choice is virtually absurd. Is the meaning of "secretary" really "helper"? What does the child learn from a task such as this?

Workbook questions are often designed without a real lesson to be learned from them. What is learned if often irrelevant, or in some cases, actually detrimental to the beginning reader. If a child begins to look for the suffix "-ary" to help him piece together the meanings of unknown words he will merely get confused. "Stations" have not more to do with "stationary," or "mercens" with "mercenary" than do "secrets" with "secretary."

Examples of another kind sometimes make learning to read more difficult by confusing the child. For example:

4. Karen *caught it* from her mother for going out in the rain without her boots.

What happened to Karen?
a. she was scolded
b. she caught a thief
c. she caught a cold

Example 4 is an attempt to teach "phrases with special meanings." Here again, new vocabulary is not best learned in this way. But, to compound the problem, something can be learned from this example that is an important part of the reading process, but is confounded and negatively reinforced here. As we noted earlier, an important part of the reading process is the making of inferences. A child must learn to make important assumptions that will serve to connect together what he has read. In this example, the inference that Karen might have caught a cold is a good one to make, but it is the wrong answer. Good readers will frequently answer Example 4 incorrectly because they have learned to make assumptions and draw conclusions. If they read quickly and are a bit sloppy in the conclusions they draw, then it is easy enough for them to get the wrong answer. At first thought, it might seem a good idea to negatively reinforce such reading habits. But, as we have seen, the process of reading depends very much on the ability to leap to conclusions, draw inferences, and in general make assumptions about what will happen. Even though leaping to conclusions will sometimes fail one in reading, such behavior is very much the basis of our ability to understand. One of the things that makes it difficult for some people to learn to read is this need to rely upon what was not in the text to help in understanding what was in the text.

Giving children the confidence to rely upon their assumptions is of great importance. Yet, as this example illustrates, many reading exercises that children are asked to do actually shake that tenuous confidence. Here, finding the correct answer requires one to read very carefully, making no chancy assumptions at all. In other words, a confident reader is likely to get in trouble here by leaping to the wrong conclusions based upon a "quick read." What is being taught here is careful, literal-minded reading, which is precisely the kind of reading that causes mediocre readers to give up in the face of complicated texts that require them to make assumptions and push on in the face of difficulty.

Another example of this is:

The farmer ate his breakfast and then fed his chickens.

   a. What three words tell what the farmer did first?
   b. What one word tells who fed the chickens?
   c. What word describes the farmer?

Here, the child is being asked to do something akin to the parsing or structural decomposition of sentences. Yet, he is not told that this is what is being asked. The child has the task of figuring out what is wanted of him. These sentences are well below the competence of an average fourth grader. He can read them with ease. But he cannot easily understand what is being asked of him. Bright children are likely to answer "breakfast, fed, chickens" to question "a." The "correct" answer is "ate his breakfast." In time, of course, the child will determine that he is often asked obvious questions for which literal answers are required. He will, at that point, have learned how to take a test. Examples such as those above teach testmanship, not reading.

USING WHAT A CHILD KNOWS

On occasion, designers of reading texts forget that children have a limited but hardly non-existent set of knowledge. There is as little point in teaching children what they already know as there is in trying to teach them what they cannot reasonably be expected to learn. We do not wish to bore children, nor go over their heads. It is important for reading workbooks to take this into account. Consider, in this regard, the following (again from a fourth grade reading workbook):

> Write "re" or "dis" in the space provided: The sign on the door said, "Do not ____ turb."

Here is a classic example of trying to teach children what they already know. If a child is not aware that "disturb" is a word and "returb" is not, he will do this incorrectly half the time, since "turb" by itself has no meaning. If he already knows the word "disturb," he has nothing new to learn.

> Circle the word closest in meaning to the underlined word: On a sketch, John drew a large hand which was not in proportion to the rest of the body.
>
> bad looking   proper size   color

Here is an example of something that is out of the range of the child's knowledge. However, the child will probably answer correctly because the other choices are awkward syntactically, and semantically silly. Nevertheless, the child may not understand what he has done, and again, might learn nothing.

We want to teach children what they will need to help them with reading comprehension. The other side of the coin is that we do not want to teach them what they do not need to know with respect to comprehension. We need not teach them explicitly what they know implicitly if such explicit knowledge will not aid reading.

DECOUPLING

We referred, in Chapter 3, to the advantages of decoupling the teaching of reading from instruction in a variety of skills normally linked together as part of the "language arts." Specifically, the skills we are referring to were given in a list in Chapter 3, that we reproduce here:

1. the use of dictionaries
2. punctuation
3. prefixes and suffixes
4. compound words
5. reading with expression
6. using an index
7. reading a diagram
8. synonyms and antonyms
9. making an outline
10. spelling
11. syllabification
12. capitalization
13. rules of grammar

Earlier we discussed some of the reasons why grammar, spelling, punctuation and capitalization were best taught as subjects entirely separate from reading. Here, we will discuss some issues related to teaching syllables, compound words, prefixes, and suffixes. We shall also discuss the problem of attempting to teach new vocabulary in the context of reading. The remaining issues will not be discussed here, since there is little to say about them except that they should be decoupled from teaching reading.

SYLLABLES

The difference between "knowing how" and "knowing that," that we discussed in Chapter 3, is relevant in deciding what skills that seem to relate to reading ought to be taught to children explicitly. One skill that relates to this distinction is the teaching of the principles of syllabification. Below is an example from a fourth grade reader:

Using Syllables to Help Read Words

Divide these unfamilliar words into syllables. This will help you pronounce the word.

tonic	timber
commence	menace
product	ticket
potion	afford
module	spiders

Why teach syllables? One possible purpose, we can imagine, is to help children figure out the meaning of a word they do not know by dividing it up into syllables whose meaning they do know. This sounds very nice in theory, but take a look at the words given above. They are taken directly from a fourth grade reader. Could you derive the meaning of them from their syllables? To help you determine this, I will present the answer, from the teachers' edition of that book, to the syllabification question:

ton ic	tim ber

com mence	men ace
prod uct	tick et
po tion	af ford
mod ule	spi ders

Consider the suffixes—"uct," "ic," "ule," "ber," "et," and "ders." They really have no meaning at all. Now consider the stems—"men," "tick," "mod," and "ton" all of which have meanings, none of which are the least bit applicable here. Children do not learn new words this way.

What else might they be attempting to teach? The standard conception is that such exercises are intended to help children to pronounce words that they do *not* know. For what purpose? To ask what they mean? Should class time be used to teach children to pronounce words so they can ask what they mean?

One possible answer is that children are being taught to be able to sound out words that they do not know by sight, but do know the meaning of. This is something that will be of very limited use. Consider the words given above. I have already pointed out that each syllable has either no meaning or an irrelevant one. Add to this the fact that these words are supposed to be outside the vocabulary of the child reading them. These two facts alone discredit the idea that the child will be able to recognize the words by sounding them out.

PREFIXES, SUFFIXES, AND COMPOUND WORDS

This brings us the the point of discussing what happens when there are pieces of words that do have meaning. Is there a point where prefixes and suffixes should be taught?

Prefixes and suffixes represent that middle ground between teaching the child what he already knows and teaching he something he cannot learn by reading. Most children already know, implicitly, the concept of prefixes and suffixes. They have, after all, been using them quite successfully in words they know, such as untie, undo, replay and so on. Suffixes such as -ed, -tion, -ish, are used by children before they normally learn to read.

They are used by children of school age in both speaking and under-standing, but here again understanding precedes production. They may not be able to tell you the formal rules, but they do know how to use them. Here again it seems foolish to teach them what they know.

However, combining two pieces of knowledge is a useful way to learn a third. There is a useful way to teach prefixes, suffixes and, by the same argument, compound words.

But, before I recommend teaching this, let me make clear what not to do. To do this I will have to discuss another significant issue, namely the teaching of new vocabulary items.

TEACHING NEW VOCABULARY

A great deal of school time is spent attempting to teach children new vocabulary items. This practice is in itself quite reasonable. A child needs to expand both his sight recognition vocabulary and his understanding vocabulary. However, as I have said, sight recognition vocabulary is dependent upon understanding vocabulary. So, the important point for the expansion of vocabulary is that the child learn to understand new words. Unfortunately, current methods of enlarging vocabulary frequently do not work. For example, the following is taken from a third grade reader:

The gorilla was *gargantuan* in size. He scared everybody.

large   happy   strong

Usually these questions are set up so that the right answer is obvious. In that case the child has the pleasure of feeling he is right. But, there is nothing requiring him to associate in his mind the new word with the word he has circled. He is being asked, after all, to determine a correct answer by using everything *but* the word to be learned. The new word is the last, least important part of the puzzle. He need never consult it. And, if he doesn't have to, he won't.

However, this is not the only problem. Even if he did learn a new word, he would be learning a very narrow, often slightly wrong meaning of that word. No two words in English are exactly synonymous. One carries connotations that another does not, or is used in circumstances where the other is not. If that were not the case, one of the words probably would have faded into obscurity. Teaching new words by the use of supposed synonyms in this manner seems both wrong and doomed to failure.

But there is a still larger problem at hand. Try this exercise, in the style of a child's reading text, on yourself:

The old man's *sagacity* was a great comfort to the town. In times of crisis, he always knew what to do.

A	friendliness	calmness	intelligence
B	wiseness	myopia	disease
C	good advice	stinginess	blindness

Imagine that you do not know the word "sagacity." Take a look at any of the three sets of answers and "circle" the right one. Now see, by whatever objective measure you have, if you have learned the new word. It will be very hard for you to use the new word in sentences that are not virtually identical to the one given above. There is a great deal more to learning a new word than just knowing a one word synonym for it. To make matters more difficult, all you know from this exercise is that you have selected the best answer. But in A, B, and C there is a best answer in each set. Any of these can be correct. But they are all quite different words. Is this any way to teach new vocabulary?

You cannot teach new vocabulary to a child by having him read the new word. It is very difficult to teach new vocabulary items in the context of reading. Of course, one can figure out what a word means in context, which means that one can get around a word one doesn't know. Surely this should be a last resort and should not be taught very seriously, much less stressed. What to do then?

The meaning of a word is its use. We cannot teach the meanings of new words apart from teaching how those words are used. The meaning of a word is not expressed by the substitution of a synonym. It is expressed by the range of possibilities of its use. Nothing less will work.

Adults frequently believe that they *do* learn new words by reading. And indeed, they sometimes do. If you encounter a word often enough, look it up in the dictionary, attempt to use it in a sentence, hear others use it, and so on, it is possible to learn a new word. But one has to work at it. New vocabulary is much more frequently acquired in listening to the spoken word. The spoken word provides a more fully developed personal context that is not likely to be very foreign to the hearer of the new word. We tend to anticipate the meanings of people we converse with, so we may have a good idea what a new word might mean. Furthermore, in a spoken context, it is possible to use the new word immediately, to sort of "test it out" in a conversational setting.

My point is that it is very difficult to learn new words by reading them. The added burden of sounding out the word compounds the task, and no opportunity for immediate use is present.

Now it is well to ask: how do young children learn new words? New names for objects are learned by children seeing their parents point to them while saying the word. The child responds, if he is paying attention, by saying the word back.

    parent: That is a cat.
    parent: What is that?
     child: Cat.

This sequence is repeated a number of times, in any number of different places, and with a number of different cats, before the child learns the word. Even then, the child is likely to call some other animal a cat and will have to be corrected. Gradually, after sufficient experience with examples of the object and the correct naming of the object, the child learns the word.

But life is not so simple. Languages have many words that do not refer to the names of objects. How are words that describe actions or attributes of objects learned? As I indicated earlier, most words of this kind are learned initially as words that describe entire situations with which the child is familiar. After the age of one and a half or so, when the child is presented with a new word in a context that he understands, the child will immediately repeat it. Children nearly automatically, after the age of two or three, repeat a new word that they have just heard, if it occurs in a context they understand. Often they will use the word in the very next sentence they say.

This repetition serves to give them a familiarity with the use of that word in a context. Thus, to teach new words one must allow them to be used immediately and orally.

COMPOUND WORDS

Now we can return to our discussion of teaching prefixes, suffixes, and compound words. Along with the notions of prefix and suffix, the idea of compound words is taught in third and fourth grade readers. Teaching compound words complicates matters by trying to do two wrong things at once: teach new vocabulary and teach children misguided principles about how words can be "figured out." Here is another example from a fourth grade reader:

After losing his third race in a row Fred was very *downhearted*.
a. low in spirits
b. tired and happy
c. having a low-placed heart

Here is a classic example of teaching nothing. Any child can correctly guess the right answer by a process of elimination. He need not pay attention to the new vocabulary item and will learn nothing.

Similarly, although it is a good idea to teach children new ideas and inform them of things that they do not know, this is hardly the way to do it. Consider another example:

In the winter, the plants in the *greenhouse* were warmed by the sun.
a. a green building

b. a place covered with grass
c. a building with lots of glass

A child who had never heard of a greenhouse could only guess at the correct answer. It requires knowing the answer, to answer correctly, since "greenhouse" is not a combination of "green" and "house."

But reading new words that are combinations of words a child already knows, used in their most common sense, is worthwhile. Examples of these are "pocketknife," "anteater," "bookshelf," and so on. They are not (again, examples taken from fourth grade readers) "hold up," "hangdog," and "touchdown."

It is easy to confuse matters and imagine that, since there is usually some connection between a compound word and its meaning, a child can figure out what the compound word means. It is helpful here to understand something of historical linguistics. Language is constantly undergoing change in a number of ways. Over time, words change in their pronounciation, for example. This is the reason that some of Shakespeare sometimes doesn't rhyme the way it once did. It is also the reason that so many words in English are spelled strangely. "Through" and "rough" were once pronounced quite similarly, for example. In the same way, words gradually change meaning. One way they do this is through metaphorical extension (e.g., the sense of "see" that means "understand," and the sense of "kill" in "the House killed the bill"). They also do this by compounding in curious ways, or in ways that reflect the history of the combination. So, "touchdown" may once have had to do with touching the ball down, and "hold up" with holding up your hands. Those are interesting facts for the student of the history of our language, but learning them will not enhance reading capabilties. A child can learn compound words as easily as any other words by encountering them in a context in which they can be used. On the other hand, it is very difficult to determine the meaning of many compound words. To see this, try to figure out for yourself the meaning of these words, assuming you knew nothing of what they meant:

bookworm
candlestick

first down
roundhouse
cowcatcher
runway
headcheese

The best object of a lesson in compound words might be to allow the child to figure out exactly what a "hard-looking" word means. In essence then, this should be a lesson in self-reliance in reading. Where the child cannot discern the correct meaning (by other than a process of elimination, in the reading text example) the idea of compound words will only be frustrating. The best lesson would reveal that it is worth giving unfamiliar words a try, since you just might be able to make sense of them.

PREFIXES AND SUFFIXES AGAIN

This, then, is also the lesson for prefixes and suffixes. You must take the prefixes and suffixes the child already knows, and combine them with roots he already knows, to allow him to realize that he can figure out what is going on. The more words a child can figure out for himself, the less frustrated he will be by reading. Here again, you are not teaching new vocabulary. You are teaching ways of dealing with an unfamiliar word.

Here are some good examples of prefix and suffix addition that are worth discussing and putting into texts for children to "figure out" while reading:

repay, untrue, uncover, misplace, unbutton, rejoin
painless, mountainous, healthful

Conversely, here are examples of words *not* to teach and ways *not* to teach them. (Again, these are taken from a fourth grade reader):

When Billie Jean hit the ball into the *forecourt*, Bobby was unable to hit it back.
a. front court

b. wrong court

c. court before

This example is meaningless to someone who doesn't know anything about tennis. In addition it is trying to teach "fore-," a prefix not in the child's vocabulary in the first place. "Forecourt" is a technical term, almost an idiom, and absolutely misplaced in a prefix lesson.

My sister, who wants to be a doctor, is taking *premedical* courses.

a. not medical

b. before medical

c. opposite of medical

We have the same problem here. We are out of the range of the child's knowledge. What is a course? Does a fourth grader know? "Premedical" is a word that the child will undoubtedly forget, having no use for it. A good guesser can be right here and yet learn nothing.

Now the argument could be made that the child is being taught to "get through" the word here, to figure out enough to be able to continue reading, *not* to learn the new word and add it to his vocabulary. Such arguments fail to appreciate the nature of a child using such a workbook. Most children want to get the right answer and move on as quickly as possible. If a child knows that "pre" means "before" he can bet the right answer. In this case he will move on to the next question. Most children are not scholars, after all. If they don't learn as a natural consequence of what they are doing, it is unlikely that they will learn at all.

SUMMING UP

The teaching of reading must be differentiated from the teaching of language skills, and both of these must be separated from the teaching of irrelevancies about language.

Children should learn how to spell, alphabetize, read diagrams, make outlines, and so on. But such lessons have nothing to do with reading and should not be coupled with reading. Such activities should be separated into those having to do with writing and thsoe that are simply useful everyday skills. Reading texts, and therefore reading groups as well, should be concerned solely with reading. Reading proceeds at its own pace and is, in the end, far more significant to our daily lives in a modern society than any of the other skills mentioned above.

Actually, the teaching of reading *should* be coupled with something external to reading, namely, the acquisition of knowledge. In the next chapter, we will discuss how this might work.

11 The Context Method

In this book I have attempted to present a view of reading instruction that treats reading as an additional facility in language, a facility that can be developed as an adjunct to the facilities that a child possesses.

At the onset of reading, the typical child functions effectively with his language. Often the teaching of reading is confused with teaching a child about his language. I have assumed in this book that reading is a new subject for the child but that comprehension is not. To teach a child to read requires concentrating on the problems in reading that are specific to reading. The most significant of these problems are: the association of sounds with printed words; the reliance on prediction and memory in the sight recognition of words; the making of inferences to add implicit facts to those explicitly mentioned; and the understanding of the role of actions and characters in a story.

Thus, reading should be taught as a subject that contains specific elements, and these elements should be taught in some sensible order. From our research in programming computers to read, we have discovered some of these elements. My approach to the teaching of reading attempts to make use of those results. My approach also assumes that since a child already knows his langauge, we should not bore him with it and thus prejudice him against reading. However, my suggestion that the teaching of language and the teaching of reading should be separated does not imply that language should not be taught at all.

I shall address the issue of the teaching of language in this chapter. In so doing I will introduce what may be a more effective method for teaching children to read—the context method.

THE TEACHING OF LANGUAGE

As I have argued previously, there is no reason to teach a child what he already knows, on the one hand, or what he will never need to know, on the other. Furthermore, there is a definite need to dissociate unrelated subjects that have been previously linked as part of a reading lesson. Whatever the need for teaching them, such subjects have no strong relationship to reading and can only confuse matters when placed in the context of reading. The question here is, which parts of language fall into which of the following four categories:

Material a Child Already Knows

Material a Child Will Never Need to Know

Material that is Useful to Know but is Unrelated to Reading

Material That is a Natural Part of What Should be Taught in the Context of Reading

To answer the question, let us examine some of the aspects of language that are currently taught within the context of reading, to see which ones fall where. In doing this, I will also discuss some lessons that are not normally taught as part of instruction in language and some that have been taught in the past but are not currently taught.

MATERIAL A CHILD ALREADY KNOWS

The first problem is assessing what a child already knows, prior to his schooling, and what he will need to know about his language apart from learning to read. The real question is: Is it possible to speak well and understand correctly, without being able to read at all? The answer to this is clearly yes. Many intelligent historical figures were illiterate. And many cultures today have no written language, yet people within those cultures speak and understand their language. It is easy to confuse literacy with the ability to function in one's culture and use one's language. This is because people who use language well are also highly likely to have been well-educated, which involves literacy. But, one should be careful to avoid a "post hoc ergo propter hoc" argument here. The ability to speak and understand one's language precedes the ability to read it, both developmentally and historically. Reading is a fairly recent phenomenon in the history of man and in most of the dominant world cultures. The ability to speak is not.

Well then, how do children learn to speak well? If they are not to be instructed in their language as part of reading, should they be instructed in their language at all?

The answer to this question is complex. First let me state that there is no need to instruct elementary school children in their language. They know, and will continue to develop, their knowledge of *how to* speak and understand their language, including the knowledge they need of syntax, semantics, and so on. This knowledge develops by usage, not by explicit instruction. Thus, it should be "taught" by placing children in situations that involve speaking. This is what is done by the parent. And it is presumably what must be done by the teacher.

My suggestions here are these: Have conversations with children in class. They should have to listen critically to what you say. After they can read a little, have them talk about what they read and hear. We teach children to use language by making them use it. The more they use it, the more facile they will become with it. Children learn language by imitation and use. Give them good models to imitate, and make them use it. Do not instruct them explicitly about nouns, predicates, antonyms or other aspects of language that they implicitly know.

Should we ever teach students about their language? I believe that language itself is a fascinating subject. Indeed the study of langauge has been the focus of my professional life. I believe that the study of language, how it works, its history and development, and so on, would be a useful part of any high school student's curriculum. Such a subject should definitely be taught in high school, but not because it will teach the student to speak, write, or read better. It will not. Rather, it should be taught because an educated person should have knowledge of language.

It is important to examine here exactly what the beginning reader already knows. He knows all about nouns, synonyms, and so on, in the sense that he uses them quite correctly. He knows more about them implicitly than researchers on language know explicitly. It is folly for us to try and teach him, when in a serious sense he is teaching us. Scientists would love to know exactly what it is that a child knows that enables him to speak and understand.

This is, after all, what we have been doing in Artificial Intelligence research. We are attempting to have machines to read the way people do, to have conversations the way people do, to write the way people do. But how do people do it? We have learned a great deal about the subject. Much of what we have learned has been illustrated by what we have been discussing here. But there is a great deal we do not know about the processes people use when they are engaged in everyday conversation, reading and writing. So, it is best not to teach children our ill-formed theories of what they are doing when they do it so well without our help.

MATERIAL A CHILD WILL NEVER NEED TO KNOW

In our zeal to teach children about their language, we have taught naive theories of language that a child implicitly knows. We have also taught naive theories of language that are very likely wrong, as well as ones for which there is not much evidence.

An example of this is instruction in syllabification, which I have discussed at length. Another classic example of a theory which is taught to young children, but that has no proven scientific validity, is the formal theory of syntax. No one has ever been able to enumerate all of the grammatical rules of English. There is good reason to believe that they have failed in this because people do not use grammatical rules in the way that certain linguists interested in syntax would have us believe. It makes no sense to teach children elaborate and difficult rules for which they have no use. Teaching transformational grammar to elementary school children is another example of just not knowing what is relevant to teach.

MATERIAL UNRELATED BUT USEFUL

I will not explore here such subjects as alphabetization, punctuation, the use of the dicitonary, and so on. As long as it is understood that such subjects must be separated from the teaching of reading, they definitely should be taught.

In this section I will discuss a subject that is of paramount importance, both because it is germane to the topic, and because it is the most heavily stressed subject in the context of reading. I am referring to the teaching of vocabulary.

I noted earlier that we rarely learn the meaning of a new word by reading it. That this should be so is obvious. We spend a tremendous amount of our time speaking and hearing. Indeed, for most people, their entire day involves using spoken language in some form or other. But written language makes up a comparatively small part of the lives of most of us. Even the most educated of people will spend more time speaking and hearing than reading or writing.

As I will discuss in Chapter 12, a basic part of our processing abilities involves skipping words we do not know or care about, while continuing to understand the gist of the matter. Children only understand a small portion of what they hear. Yet they push on. Eventually, when they are ready to pay attention to a new word, they can ask about it or figure out what it means. But, let me emphasize, this only happens for a comparatively small percentage of the new words that they encounter.

The same is true for reading. When a child discovers a new word in the course of reading, he usually finds it much easier to skip it than learn its meaning. When the child completely understands the context that surrounds a word, in the sense of having predicted its meaning, he can then learn the word by reading it. On the other hand, when a new word is spoken by a friend or teacher, used a second or third time, and finally used by the child himself, it will be possible to learn the word. This is a key point. A combination of reading and usage will result in the learning of new vocabulary. But the child has to use the word, in writing or conversation, a number of times in order truly to learn it.

Of course, adults can, if they bother, go to a dictionary, look up a word, and memorize it. However, they are usually reluctant to use such a word, and are likely to forget it and thus have to repeat the process. New vocabulary must be introduced verbally, in a conversation or story, and repeated over and over again. The child must be encouraged to use the new word and respond to others using it.

Can we teach new vocabulary in school? I believe we can and must. The "how" of the matter is crucial, and this I shall discuss in the next section.

MATERIAL THAT IS PART OF THE CONTEXT OF READING

The watchword throughout this book has been *knowledge*. The acquisition of knowledge about the world is the single most important part of reading. You cannot read about that which makes no sense to you. To prove this point to yourself, try reading a folktale, in English, taken from a culture very removed from yours. A classic in this regard is "The War of the Ghosts," an Eskimo folktale. Psychologists have demonstrated that this particular story is very hard to remember (or read), as are all stories for which one does not possess the appropriate background knowledge.

> One night two young men from Egulac went down to the river to hunt seals, and while they were there it became foggy and calm. Then they heard

war-cries, and they thought, "Maybe this is a war-party." They escaped to the shore, and hid behind a log. Now canoes came up, and they heard the noise of paddles, and saw one canoe coming up to them. There were five men in the canoe, and they said,

"What do you think? We wish to take you along. We are going up the river to make war on the people."

One of the young men said, "I have no arrows." "I will not go along. I might be killed. My relatives do not know where I have gone. But you," he said, turning to the other, "may go with them."

So one of the young men went, but the other returned home.

And the warriors went on up the river to a town on the other side of Kalama. The people came down to the water, and they began to fight, and many were killed. But presently the young man heard one of the warriors say, "Quick, let us go home; that Indian has been hit." Now he thought, "Oh, they are ghosts." He did not feel sick, but they said he had been shot.

So the canoes went back to Egulac, and the young man went ashore to his house, and made a fire. And he told everybody and said, "Behold, I accompanied the ghosts, and we went to fight. Many of our fellows were killed, and many of those who attacked us were killed. They said I was hit, and I did not feel sick."

He told it all, and then he became quiet. When the sun rose he fell down. Something black came out of his mouth. His face became contorted. The people jumped up and cried.

He was dead.

This story is understandable if you "know" certain Eskimo "facts," such as:

When people die their soul, which is black, comes out of their mouths.
When ghosts shoot you, you do not feel it.

Without these facts, the story is quite confusing.

Children face a similar situation in reading. They need to have background facts at hand, and to fill them in, so as to connect the sentences. But there seems to be a certain paradox here. We use knowledge in order to read, but don't we read in order to gain knowledge? Isn't that one of the main reasons for teaching children to read?

I have attempted to treat this paradox within the progression of stages given earlier. After children learn how to fill in the implicit details of a story, and to track characters' goals and plans, they are prepared to acquire knowledge via reading. In other words, the basic background knowledge that they possess is used to help them learn to read stories that track plans and goals. The general knowledge of why people do things and how they do them can then be used to help them gain new knowledge about different goals and plans that are unfamiliar to them.

For example, once we understand about greed and the law, we can read about pirates and learn about them by reading. With our new knowledge of pirates, we can expand in both breadth and depth. We can learn about other kinds of criminals by using our knowledge about pirates, and we can learn more about pirates.

The next stage, after plans, goals, and scripts have been thoroughly learned, as they apply to reading, is to teach children to reason, draw analogies, relate one experience to another, and in general learn to assess what is happening in a situation and why it is happening. This is best done within what I shall term "the context method."

THE CONTEXT METHOD

Instruction in new vocabulary and new knowledge must be done within an overall context that is of interest to the child. The context method involves teaching other subjects to the child, apart from reading per se. Reading, new vocabulary, and so on, are taught within an overall context that provides new knowledge about a considerable range of phenomena covered by the context. Thus knowledge associated with the terminology of the new context is taught, regardless of whether or not any particular sentence to be read about that context contains that word. The new knowledge that is acquired can then be used to enhance reading. Three contexts that naturally lend themselves to the teaching of reading in this way are history, geography, and science. Others can be used as well, but these will suffice for examples.

To return to the pirate example, the history and geography contexts can be extremely useful in learning, and hence reading, about pirates. Tell the students why pirates existed, what their lives were like, where they plied their trade, what the times were like, and so on. In this context, the vocabulary of pirating will be taught naturally. Some of this vocabulary is out of date and of little use outside of pirate stories. But many words, such as "treasure," "chest," "mast," "sails," "sloop," "coast," "cove," "pistol," and so on, are in use today. To learn these words, the children must be taught to put themselves in the pirates' place, so to speak. Presented with the problem of where to anchor a ship, how to choose victims, how to avoid arrest, and so on, children find these words and concepts of vital interest. If they get to discuss their ideas, then new vocabulary is quickly acquired. (Remember, new vocabulary is best acquired aurally [and orally].) When they learn to plan as a pirate would in a given situation, given his goals, they are learning to be able to read stories about pirates, for the reasons discussed earlier.

A unit about pirates, which might require an hour a day for a month or so, would offer instruction in a number of subjects. It would also prepare children to read fairly complex stories about pirates (in which they might now have a vital interest) and give them the needed vocabulary, and a model of how and why pirates behave the way they do.

To reinforce what they are learning about pirates, plays can be written and acted out; math problems can be given within the realm of the pirate world; the children can attempt to build and sail a model pirate ship, and so on. This may seem a strange way to teach reading, but when all these things have been done, most children should be only too eager to learn whatever they can about pirates.

From a unit on pirates, a unit on Caribbean history could be developed, or one on hijacking of airplanes. In either case, current news stories would now be of more interest. Here again the same unit approach might be used. This time, however, instruction in generalization or reasoning from analogous circumstances would further enhance understanding.

Other subjects, such as science, can be taught in the same manner. A child who can learn the language of science, and who has familiarity with its methods, can also read about science. I once had the occasion to bring my four year old son to an undergraduate class I was teaching. He happened to notice the computer terminal in the room and began to talk about how he was going to "log on," when to do a "control C," or a "SYS," how to "run a program," and so on. The students in the class were astounded. But there was nothing astounding about it. As the son of a Professor of Computer Science, he of course knew all about computer terminals and had picked up the appropriate terminology from his attempts to acquire a working knowledge of how to use them. I did not present him with an elementary school level computer programming text; they do not currently exist to my knowledge. But he was capable of reading such a text. And that is exactly the point.

A child who sees a simple experiment in chemistry conducted in front of him, assuming his interest is excited by a good presentation, will quickly learn such words as "experiment," "procedure," "method," "instruments," "chemical," and so on. If he's allowed to participate directly in experiments, he will learn these words that much better. If this kind of first-hand experience happens frequently, then the words describing the experiment will become second nature to him. This is how to "teach" new vocabulary.

That child is now ready to read elementary science books. He can be helped to generalize from one experimental situation to the next. Again he will naturally acquire vocabulary and knowledge.

SUMMING UP

The context method is how reading must be taught. Reading is not just reading per se. It is reading about different subjects or within different knowledge areas. The context method of reading emphasizes the acquisition of new knowledge first. This new knowledge brings with it a new vocabulary, which is easily added to the child's sight-recognition vocabulary. Knowledge of the whole situation enables the child to make the necessary connections in the text, so he can gain *new* knowledge. All of these together, with one final ingredient, are what comprise reading.

The final ingredient is interest. As long as the child cares about what he is reading, he will happily read—if he has the requisite background knowledge.

12 Commencement: How It All Works

During the course of this book, I have attempted to introduce three topics. First, I have been presenting, albeit in a rather modified form, a theory of language that my colleagues and I have been developing over the last ten years or so. Second, I have been relying on results obtained from testing that theory of language on computers. The tests have been aimed at making computers literate. During the course of writing those computer programs, we have continually modified our theories about how people process language. We have made these modifications whenever one of our proposals simply would not work because of a flaw in the logic of the procedure. Much of what I have discussed here comes from that work.

The third thing I have been discussing, obviously, is the potential relationship between the teaching of reading to children and the teaching of reading to computers.

In this chapter I would like to provide the reader with an overall view of how the reading process works, both in people and in one of the computer models we have built. I present this by way of a conclusion to this book, but it is by no means conclusive. The model I will now present is one on which we are currently working. This chapter is thus a sort of commencement, or beginning of things.

MODELING A READER

Let's consider how a normal, literate adult reads a story. One important point to notice about people when they are reading is that they are very fast. We have dwelt at length in this book on the wealth of inferencing and tying-in of relevant background knowledge, as well as other problems that one must deal with in the course of understanding a written or a spoken sentence. People are constantly tracking goals and plans, applying scripts, and making an enormous number of inferences. Yet, when a sentence is completed, they have finished processing it. People understand very quickly, considering the fact that they finish understanding, for the most part, as soon as the sentence they are hearing has finished being uttered. This implies that they do not for the initial decoding of the meaning of the sentence to be completed before they begin the process of inferencing and applying knowledge. Rather, all the processing that we have talked about must be occurring on as each individual word is read. That is, people must be making inferences based upon the early parts of a sentence, *before* they even hear the latter parts of the sentence. If this is so, then it also follows that people will make use of information found in the course of processing, thus allowing things such as word sense identification to be affected by higher-level processes. People cannot be making a syntactic analysis of a sentence and then be sending their results off to an inferencer. They must do all their processing work, following goals and so on, as the words are input to them, one by one.

It does not necessarily follow from this that people always read in the same way. Indeed, in speed-reading courses people are often taught to read in a manner quite different from the one word at a time method. But, in normal reading, people process words one at a time, left to right. They do not wait for an end of a sentence before they begin processing that sentence. They use their knowledge to formulate predictions that help them process as they read. These predictions are not always conscious. For example, when a person is reading a story and comes to the end of a page in mid-sentence, it is quite common to be able to predict what the rest of the sentence will be like. The predictions that a reader makes in mid-sentence are made because they help to process the rest of that sentence.

There is a further consequence to this view of processing. If all this extra processing must take place, that is, if inferring is added to initial meaning decoding, knowledge assessment, and so on, the processing time probably is not allocated equally. Some words are likely to excite more processing than others. But, in spoken language at least, and in written language read at a constant rate of speed, each word takes as much time to hear or see as the next. That is, a speaker doesn't pause after the word that excites lots of inferences; he keeps on going. Time must be found to do this extra processing, which will be at the expense of something else. This something else is likely to be some less interesting word, as not all words have equal import. Some words require a lot of processing time (those that have great syntactic, semantic, or inferential importance, for example), while others are hardly noticed.

It is obvious that people cannot be fully processing every word they hear. What is more likely that case is that as they listen, they decide what needs serious attention and what needs less attention (although a reader is usually not aware that he has made such decisions). Such decisions can be explained on the basis of many factors. The most obvious one is interest. People are liable to pay attention to (that is, devote their processing time to) what interests them.

Consider the following sentence:

A small twin-engine airplane carrying federal marshals and a convicted murderer who was being transported to Leavenworth crashed during an emergency landing at O'Hare Airport yesterday.

It seems obvious that some parts of this sentence are more interesting than others. But more than that, it is crucial, according to the idea stated above, with respect to the amount of processing time available, that the processing of some words take less time than it does to read or hear them.

Now at first glance this may seem a bit bizarre. How can a word be processed in less time than it takes to read or hear it, if reading or hearing it is a part of that processing? Yet we are in precisely this paradoxical situation if we hold to the idea that the processing of any one word in a sentence can take longer than the time it takes to read or hear it. This must be the case, however, since it takes no longer to process an entire sentence that it does to hear it, and since the individual words are spoken at such a rate that there is no time between them in which to process. (This is obviously the case since just finding the word boundaries in a spoken sentence is a very complex task, because the speech stream is continuous.) The connection with reading here is yet to be proved. But, it would seem obvious that humans who have developed methods for handling the speech stream might employ those methods in reading as well. It is unlikely that we have two very different mechanisms available for decoding langauge.

Thus some words demand more processing time than others. Since the amount of available processing time is limited by the rate of flow of the input (which is continuous for speech), then some words must not be processed at all (or in any case, they are processed so minimally that they are hardly seen). One hypothesis is that the understanding process may not be entirely left to right. Since the most important words often come at the end of a phrase, the preceding words may be virtually ignored until they can be "gathered up" right to left. By right to left, we mean that while the stream of input is obviously from left to right, words are stored in memory and barely processed until a word that initiates processing is found. When such a word is found, the words stored in memory are gathered up and placed in their conceptual slots.

In order to process the kind of noun phrase that begins the first sentence in the above story, we must assume that a processor barely processes any words until it reaches "airplane." Instead, it simply marks the existence of the first four words in short term memory for retrieval after the main noun is encountered. Once we know that "airplane" is the subject of the sentence, expectations can be generated that allow us to have a better idea of what to look for. For example, "carrying" will barely be processed here because, although we are only beginning to recognize what word it is, we have already heard about the marshals and the murderer and have decided to pay attention to those items. This kind of "partial processing" has the advantage of not bogging us down in difficult problems such as trying to find the right sense of "carrying." This can be determined later when more information about the context is known.

The point here is that we are really not seeing things one word at a time. Rather, we are seeing a continuous stream of words, from which we can select what we find interesting, return to discover just those relationships that connect together what we are interested in while virtually ignoring the rest. Do we care that the verb "carrying" was used instead of "containing," or that the construction used was not "in which they were flying"? Evidence suggests that people cannot recall such word-based information after a small amount of time. One explanation for this is that they weren't paying much attention to such information in the first place.

AN EXAMPLE

To see how this works in reality, consider the following sentence from the front page story in the *New York Times*. Let me lead you through the sentence in a kind of slow-motion view of the processing decisions that must be made in order to understand its meaning:

> An Arabic speaking gunman shot his way into the Iraqi Embassy here (Paris) yesterday morning, held hostages through most of the day before surrendering to French policeman and then was shot by Iraqi security officials as he was led away by the French officers.

We will now examine this sentence word by word and consider the kind of processing that it requires.

One important point here is that although we will discuss this sentence in a left to right, word-by-word fashion, there is no real reason to assume that actual processing proceeds one word at a time. Actually, words enter in chunks, both visually (in reading) and aurally (in speech). In this discussion, I refer to a dictionary. By this I mean a mental dictionary that contains processing information for any word we encounter (as was discussed in Chapter 4). This information includes both what the word means and some suggestions about what to look for after it has been encountered

What follows is an English description of how one of our computer programs (called IPP, see Schank, Lebowitz, and Birnbaum, 1979; Lebowitz, 1979) actually works. This particular program is designed to read newspaper stories and to model human memory processing as it does so.

An Arabic speaking gunman . . .

AN is a word that can be skipped initially. This means that when it is looked up in the dictionary, what is found there are instructions to go to the next word and place AN in some kind of short term memory (STM) to be examined later.

ARABIC is listed in the dictionary as a word that is skippable when it has been preceded by a skippable word, so it is skipped and placed in STM. In general, adjectives can be skipped, though this is not true for all adjectives. In particular, "Russian" could not be skipped, because it can also be a noun. Also, interesting adjectives may not be skipped (i.e., "disgusting," "murderous," "lecherous").

SPEAKING can also be skipped as long as no potential actors have been encountered so far. A search for ACTORs in STM finds none, so this word is also skipped.

GUNMAN is marked as an ACTOR, as a NOUN, and as a HIGH INTEREST ACTOR. The fact that we have a HIGH INTEREST word causes us to begin to try to fill in certain information. In particular, we now want to know the answers to the following questions:

> WHO is he?—causes us to gather up the adjectives we have seen so far and add them to what we know about this GUNMAN
>
> WHAT did he do?—this is answered by an item found in what we know about this GUNMAN, namely SHOOT. Thus, an inference that the gunman shot or will

shoot somebody is made here before anything
else comes in as input
WHO did he shoot?—causes us to be interested in the syntactic object
of the verb, which we assume will be SHOOT
WHY did he shoot?—causes us to look for a reason
WHERE did this happen?—causes us to look for a location
WHAT SCRIPTS might
this initiate?—GUNMAN can itself cause a script to be called
in to help us in processing. Prime candidates are
the ROBBERY script, the TERRORIST script,
and the KIDNAP script. We can now look for
confirmation in the rest of the sentence.

The formulation of the above questions now guides the analysis of the
rest of this sentence. The answers to these questions are what is of interest
to the understander. Thus these questions guide meaning extraction,
syntactic issues, script application, inferencing, tracking goals, and so on,
all at once.

shot his way into the Iraqi Embassy . . .

SHOT is encountered and immediately is found to satisfy an expectation that was derived from GUNMAN. Satisfying an expectation of this
sort is the way that conceptual structures are built, and we now build the
first one, namely, an APPLY FORCE action with "bullets" as object;
"gun" as the originating direction, the gunman as actor, and an unfilled
final direction for the bullets. This unfilled slot is marked as the same one
that satisfies the answer to the WHO question raised previously. The
reader will now look for the answer by looking for the next main noun in
the next noun phrase.

HIS is skipped and held in STM as before.

WAY does not satisfy the expectation to fill the empty slot. WAY is
also listed as both "skippable" and pointing to a direction or location. We
now start to look for that location.

INTO tells us to keep on going, and it is temporarily skipped.

THE is placed in memory.

IRAQI is placed in memory.

EMBASSY is found to be a location and is set up as the location needed by the APPLY FORCE. Furthermore, EMBASSY is marked as interesting and a place of political significance. This latter piece of information satisfies the expectation for initiating the TERRORIST script that we had predicted (among others) from GUNMAN. Since EMBASSY is interesting, expectations deriving from it are aroused. One of these is for the country that maintains the EMBASSY. IRAQI is thus found in STM where it was previously placed and it is picked up.

Setting up the TERRORIST script causes us to expect answers to the following questions:
Were HOSTAGES taken?
What demands were made? (money?) (free political prisoners?)
Was any damage done?
What measures to counteract the terrorist were made? (return fire; arrest; free hostages)
here yesterday morning . . .
HERE, when used in a news story, instructs us to add the location mentioned in the dateline to the location slot.

YESTERDAY is found to be a time word and is thus added to the time slot of the event.

MORNING is also handled in this manner.

held hostages through most of the day . . .

HELD is skipped, since it matches none of our previously established expectations. It matches none of them because the information found about HELD in the part of the dictionary we consult at this point is just that it is a verb. No verbs were needed, so we skip it. This could have changed if there were some interest-value marking or other item of significance. The advantages of not immediately attempting to assess its meaning are significant. HELD is a highly ambiguous word, but we need not make any decision about it right away. The reason for this can be seen in what happens in subsequent processing of this phrase.

HOSTAGES is immediately found to satisfy an expectation. The TAKE HOSTAGES scene of the TERRORIST script is initiated. At this point a check is made on the verb that has been placed in memory (HELD) to see if doing this is all right. If the verb were "shot," for example this initiation would not work. HELD is found to be precisely the kind of word that fits here. The important point is that HELD never really had to be examined for its meaning, which is helpful because words like HELD really do not have any particular meaning. Its meaning is derived from its connection to HOSTAGES, and HOSTAGES is comprehensible only through the TERRORIST script. This is a very important point with respect to how people read. You need not fully process every word to find its meaning. Indeed, such processing often just impedes understanding.

THROUGHOUT is found to point to either a time or place, so a word indicating time or place is expected. However, a reader knows, at this point, what his interests are. In particular, satisfying the expectations that are still active is very important, because they are death-related expectations, and that is a subject which is of great interest to humans. Thus we virtually ignore the rest of this phrase due to lack of interest.

MOST is placed in STM.

OF is also placed in STM.

THE is held until it might be needed.

DAY is placed in memory. It also satisfies the low-level expectation for a time word, and this information is added to what we know about time and will be used later if we become interested in what we have now decided is uninteresting.

before surrendering to French policemen . . .

BEFORE is a time-ordering word that prepares us to set up a new event and mark its time relative to the preceding event.

SURRENDERING is a word that is marked as of high interest and as part of a number of scripts including TERRORIST. The surrender scene of the TERRORIST script is initiated and expectations are aroused, concerning the reasons for this action, his captors, etc. Certain words are marked as indicating which of these might follow. Thus "because" marks off reasons, and "to" marks off captors.

TO tells us that captors is coming.

FRENCH is held in memory.

POLICEMEN is marked as a noun that can be an ACTOR, so STM is consulted to gather up its relevant components. POLICEMAN also is a possible captor (because it it both a human and an institution, either of which would do), so it satisfies two of our previous expectations.

and then was shot by Iraqi security officials . . .

AND says a new event is coming whenever an event has just ended.

THEN orders the time of the event.

WAS specifies that the actor stored in STM is the conceptual object of the new event. This sets up expectations for the actor and the action.

SHOT is found to be interesting. It is also expected because it is the action we have been predicting from a GUNMAN. Thus we have:

WHO did he shoot?—GUNMAN
WHO shot?—not answered
WHY did he shoot?—not answered
WHERE did this happen?—already known
WHAT SCRIPTS does this instantiate?—

> SHOOT can also cause a script to be instantiated. Prime candidates are ROBBERY, TERRORIST, and KID-NAP, ordinarily. But we are in a context set up by TERRORIST. None of the above are normal continuations of TERRORIST. This causes us to look for plans and goals.

WHAT were the RESULTS of this actions?—

> A expectation is set up to find the results. If this expectation is not satisfied, the usual results of this action are inferred—in this case, death for the object.

Since SHOT is interesting we need to explain it. No scripts are available here, so we need to ask who would want to kill the GUNMAN and why. These expectations are added to the active expectations.

BY tells us to go on.

IRAQI is skipped and stored.

SECURITY is skipped and stored.

OFFICIALS is used to end the processing of the noun group. It satisfies the expectations for WHO did the shooting and, as we now have an actor, we ask why they would kill a TERRORIST. This causes us to examine the knowledge we have about why TERRORISTS might be killed after capture. We have none directly on hand. This causes us to be surprised by this event. We seek to explain it by using a REVENGE or SHUT HIM UP belief, but we are only guessing at this point.

as he was led away by French officers . . .

We are basically done now, as no further expectations need to be satisfied immediately. (We know this after we have seen a period and have found no new expectations.) We are still interested in the goals of each of the actors however, so "because" expectations are still active.

AS is known to be a time co-occurrence word. Since we are not interested in anything that occurred at the same time, unless it is itself interesting, we can now skip ahead and look for actions or actors that are interesting.

HE is skipped.

WAS is skipped.

LED is uninteresting and is both noticed and then skipped.

AWAY is skipped.

BY is skipped.

THE is skipped.

FRENCH is skipped.

OFFICERS is skipped because there are no expectations that relate to it.

The period tells us we are done.

The final representation for this sentence is:

TERRORISM
    ACTOR—Arab gunman
    PLACE— Paris Iraqi Embassy

```
SCENES
  HOSTAGES—some
  CAPTURE
    ACTOR— French policemen
    OBJECT—Arab gunman
    PLACE— Iraqi Embassy
UNEXPECTED RESULT:  ACTOR—Iraqi officers
                    ACTION—APPLY FORCE
                    OBJECT—Arab gunman
                    ITEM—bullets
                    DIRECTION (FROM)—gun
                    RESULT
                      ACTOR—Arab gunman
                      STATE—dead
```

I have given the final representation for the story as it is output by our computer program. We assume that people have some internal representation of the story that corresponds to that given above. Since my point here was to illustrate something of what the details of understanding are like, I will not bother with the complexities of the above representation. Our programs use that representation to translate the sentence they have read, to answer questions about it, make paraphrases, and so on. Any reader of that story would need to have retained the information shown above, but not the information that was left out.

It is the decoding of English into these kinds of meaning representations that constitutes understanding. Reading is the process of decoding. To do this we need a great deal of knowledge. This knowledge is primarily about the world, and secondarily about how such information can be found in the linguistic code. As for issues of language as language, in terms of the pure form of language, such information is just a very small part of the overall picture. To teach reading one must teach the process of decoding a sentence to an underlying meaning representation.

We have ended as we have started then, with the attempt to program computers to read. The program described above performs rather well when it has the relevant background knowledge. What we have learned about reading, from it and other programs we have written, has taught us a great deal. Much of what we have learned is relevant to teaching children to read. Reading is a complex and fascinating process to study scientifically. But, it is important that it be simple and fascinating for the beginning reader.

References

Anderson, J., (1974) Verbatim and propositional representation of sentences in immediate and long term memory. *Journal of Verbal Learning and Verbal Behavior*, Vol. 13, pps. 149–162.

Benedict, H., (1976) *Language Comprehension in 10 to 16 Month-old Infants*. (thesis) Department of Psychology, Yale University, New Haven, Conneticut.

Carbonell, J., (1979) Subjective Models of Belief Systems. Research Report #150, Department of Computer Science, Yale University.

Cullingford, R. E., (1978) Script Application: Computer Understanding of Newspaper Stories. Research Report #116, Department of Computer Science, Yale University.

Goodman, K. (1967) Reading: A Psycholinguistic Guessing Game. *Journal of the Reading Specialist* Vol. 6, pps. 126–135.

Nelson, K. (1975) Cognitive Development and the Acquisition of Concepts. Paper presented at the Conference on Schooling and the Acquisition of Knowledge, San Diego.

Nelson, K. and Gruendel, J. (1978) From person episode to social script: two dimensions in the development of event knowledge. Paper presented at the Biennial meeting of the Society for Research in Child Development, San Francisco.

Piaget, J. (1954) *The Child's Construction of Reality*. Basic Books, New York.

Sachs, J. S. (1967) Recognition memory for syntactic and semantic aspects of connected discourse. *Perception and Psychophysics*, Vol. 2, pps. 437–442.

Schank, R. C. (1973) Identification of conceptualizations underlying natural language. In R. C. Schank and K. Colby, eds. *Computer Models of Thought and Language*. W. H. Freeman, San Francisco.

Schank, R. C. (1975) *Conceptual Information Processing*. North Holland, Amsterdam.

Schank, R. C. (1975) The structure of episodes in memory. In D. Bobrow and T. Collins, (eds.) *Representation and Understanding: Studies in Cognitive Science*. Academic, New York.

Schank, R. C. and Abelson, R. P. (1977) *Scripts Plans Goals and Understanding*. Lawrence Erlbaum Associates, Hillsdale, New Jersey.

Schank, R. C., (1978) Interestingness: Controlling Inferences. Research Report #145, Department of Computer Science, Yale University.

Schank, R., Lebowitz, M., and Birnbaum, L. (1980) An Integrated Understander. *American Journal of Computational Linguistics*. Vol. 6, No. 1, pps. 13–30.

Selfridge, M. G. (1980) A Process Model of Language Acquisition. Research Report #172, Department of Computer Science, Yale University.

Wetstone, H. S. and Friedlander, B. Z. (1973) Effect of Word Order on Young Children's Responses to Simple Questions and Commands. *Child Development, 44,* 734–740.

Wilensky, R. (1978) Understanding Goal-Based Stories. Research Report #140, Department of Computer Science, Yale University.